ANATOMY OF THE SHIP

The Flower Class Corvette
AGASSIZ

ANATOMY OF THE SHIP

The Flower Class Corvette
AGASSIZ

CONWAY

JOHN McKAY & JOHN HARLAND

Frontispiece
Convoy duty on the North Atlantic – corvette *Battleford* in heavy seas. *Captain B D L Johnson Collection, courtesy of the Vancouver Maritime Museum*

© John McKay and John Harland 1993

First published in 1993 by Conway Maritime Press

This edition first published in 2004 by
Conway
an imprint of Anova Books Ltd
10 Southcombe Street
London W14 0RA
www.conwaypublishing.com

9 8 7 6 5 4 3

All rights reserved. No part of this book may be reproduced or transmitted in any form without prior written permission from the publisher.

A CIP catalogue record for this book is available from the British Library.

ISBN 10: 0 85177 975 1
ISBN 13: 9780851779751

Printed by Toppan Leefung, China

CONTENTS

ACKNOWLEDGEMENTS 6

INTRODUCTION 7
Evolution of the Flower class 8
Operational history of the HMCS *Agassiz* 10
Modifications 11
Hull form and construction 12
Superstructure 12
Accommodation 13
Machinery and bunkers 13
Steering gear 14
Anchor windlass 14
Armament 14
Minesweeping equipment 15
Asdic and radar 16
Liferafts and boats 17
Colour scheme 17
Notes for modelmakers 17
Appendix: Construction list 18

THE PHOTOGRAPHS 19

THE DRAWINGS 33
A. General arrangement 34
B. Internal hull 58
C. Construction 90
D. Machinery 108
E. Spars and rigging 124
F. Fittings 126
G. Armament 135
H. Ship's boat 146
I. Modified Flower and Castle class
   corvettes 148

SOURCES 160

ACKNOWLEDGEMENTS

Acknowledgements

Research for this project overlapped our previous collaboration *Catchers and Corvettes*, and many of those acknowledged in that book should be recognised here as well. We owe a special debt to Ken Macpherson and Marc Milner, who generously shared with us material gathered for their own book on the Canadian corvette, which will be published by Vanwell Publishing of St Catherines, Ontario, in 1993. In particular, it was an enormous bonus to us to be given access to Ken's unrivalled collection of photographs, some of which are reproduced in this book.

We also wish to thank:

John Lambert, whose drawings were of particular assistance in our illustration of corvette armament; David K Brown RCNC and Fred Walker, for resolving various problems to do with ship design; James B Lamb, who read the first draught of the Introduction; Duncan Leslie, who showed us around *Sackville*'s engine room and patiently explained a multitude of technical matters; Frank Moore, who resolved several engineering problems for us; Maurice D Smith, who introduced us to the archives of the Collingwood and Port Arthur shipyards, now held in the Marine Museum at Kingston, Ontario; Len McCann, for his help and encouragement in many ways since the beginning of the project, along with Jim Delgado; Adrian Osler, who arranged access to the model corvette engine in the attic of the Museum of Science & Industry in Newcastle-upon-Tyne; David H Roberts, who helped the project forward in several ways and gave his permission for the use of material previously published in *Catchers and Corvettes*; and Phil Thomas, who provided us with drawings of HMS *Aubretia* and other items. The South Bank yard of Smith's Dock is long since laid down, but we acknowledge with gratitude the help on many technical points provided to us by former officials of that company, notably Roger Spence and Tom Pearce.

In Canada, we profitted from conversations with Desmond W Piers and James C Hibberd, both of whom commanded escort groups in the darkest days of the early 1940s, and both of whom went on to distinguished careers and the attainment of flag rank in the RCN. We were also aided in one way or another by Alec Barbour, Alex Bone, Charles Butterworth, Eric Claggett, A G Cockle, N Roger Cole, Helen De Roia, R L Donaldson, Tony German, Michael Hadley, Joe Marston, Fraser McKee, James B Lamb, Vernon Howland, Earl Moorhead, Jack Muir, A J C Pomeroy, Peter Robertson, Andrew Rodger, Tony Storrs, Roland H Webb and Michael Whitby. In the United States we acknowledge the assistance of Alan Easton and Robert Erwin Johnson.

Through the Flower Class Corvette Association and its redoubtable president Cyril J ('Stevo') Stephens, and Jack F Williams of the Ex-*Algerine* Association, we were put in contact with Cyril Bramzell, J S Brown, C Alfred Burton, Paul Castleton, W T Chatterton, Tom Coleman, F A Dark, John N Davis, Hugh W Drake, Jack M Fairbrass, Ernie D Fleming, Teddy George, Tom Hand, Ken Hawkridge, Charles Hill, A L Lodge, J Mather, R E Moreton, Frank S Pewter, S C Reid, John Richardson, Stan Sharp, Ken Slater, F C Smith, G P Thornley and Brian Wainwright in the United Kingdom and Leo Bischoff, George M Coetzee, S M Glencross and J Linford in South Africa.

Also from South Africa came help from Richard Robinson and Peter R Humphries. In Australia, Commodore Tom Fisher unearthed a treasure for us in the form of a drawing of the minesweeping winch found on *Bathurst* class minesweepers. We also had help from Ian Carver, Tom Collingridge, John V Gibson and R J Hardstaff.

Again in the United Kingdom, Jim Colledge, John English, Arnold Hague and Bob Ruegg, all authors on corvettes or the Battle of the Atlantic, answered several enquiries each, and we also received help on technical matters from E M S Windridge and Dan Nicholson of the Royal Navy. From the Continent came help from Siegfried Bär, Wolfgang Bohlayer and Dr Dieter Jung (Germany) and Frank Abelsen, Dag Bakka and Stein Moen (Norway).

We are indebted to the following institutions:

Directorate of History, Department of National Defence, Ottawa (Dr Alec Douglas); Canadian Navy Memorial Trust and HMCS *Sackville* (Vernon Howland); the National Maritime Museum; Kirkleatham Old Hall Museum, Redcar (Bryan Booker); the Marine Museum of the Atlantic (David B Flemming and Graham McBride); the Marine Museum of the Great Lakes at Kingston; Vancouver Maritime Museum; the Museum of Science & Industry, Newcastle; the Public Archives of Canada; Societé Historique Pierre de Saurel, Sorel PQ; the Royal Canadian Military Institute, Toronto; and the Marinmuseet, Horten, Norway.

We gratefully acknowledge the contribution of Julian Mannering, Robert Gardiner and the staff at Conway Maritime Press, without whose expertise this book would not have seen the light of day. Finally, we wish to thank our wives Janet Harland and Ellen McKay for their support and exemplary patience during the course of this project.

INTRODUCTION

The subject of this book is a Flower class corvette built in Vancouver and commissioned in January 1941. *Agassiz* (pronounced Aga-see) in her as-built, short forecastle configuration differed considerably from the common conception of the long-forecastle 'Flower', such as the museum ship HMCS *Sackville* in Halifax, Nova Scotia, or the Greek corvette *Kriezis* (ex-*Coreopsis*) which represented HMS *Compass Rose* in the film *The Cruel Sea*, or 1/72 scale models from the popular Matchbox/Revell kit.

It was, however, the short-forecastle configuration that was in the mind's eye of Nicholas Monsarrat when he wrote *The Cruel Sea*, *HM Corvette*, *East Coast Corvette* and others, and this version best represents the Canadian Flowers as they were flung into the thick of the bitter Atlantic convoy battles of 1941–2, described in James Lamb's *The Corvette Navy* and Alan Easton's *50 North: Canada's Atlantic Battleground*.

In 1939, like the other combatants, Canada plunged into a war for which her naval staff were ill prepared. Despite the U-boat campaign waged by Germany in World War I, little attention had been paid in the 1920s and 1930s to the problems of anti-submarine warfare, since it was widely believed that the future threat to merchantmen would come from surface raiders and from aircraft. The RCN had investigated the possibility of building escorts based on the handsome RN *Halcyon* class sloops, but these plans had not reached fruition by the time hostilities broke out. The timely arrival of plans for a 'Patrol Vessel of Whaler Type' from the British Admiralty in 1939 thus offered a solution to a very serious weakness in Canadian naval preparations for the new war. The corvette (as the new vessel became known) was widely seen as a stopgap until more sophisticated escorts were available, but in the event was built in great numbers.

There was some confusion in Ottawa about the role the new vessels should play in the war at sea. Certainly it was completely unforeseen that at an early stage the corvettes would carry the brunt of mid-ocean convoy escort duties. How this situation arose, and how it was resolved, have been analysed thoroughly in Milner's *The North Atlantic Run*. The initial assumption was that corvettes would be used only in coastal waters, and might on occasion be engaged in sweeping contact mines. In the event, both suppositions proved false, but they explain the differences between the early Canadian corvettes and those built at the same time in Britain.

By 1941 the U-boat campaign against the convoys was in full swing, and Canada's desperate need for deep ocean escorts resulted in the pressing into service of vessels like *Agassiz*, which were barely up to the task assigned to them. Designed to be used in the short seas found in British coastal waters, and just over 200ft overall, the corvettes were quickly found to lack sufficient length to be really efficient fighting ships in the long swells of the North Atlantic. As for the employment of corvettes as minesweepers, some British corvettes did engage in limited sweeping in the Mediterranean, but Canadian corvettes, and for that matter the majority of Canadian *Bangor* and *Algerine* class minesweepers, were used entirely as escorts. The minesweeping gear proved an encumbrance in their role as convoy escorts, and was eventually removed.

When the first Canadian corvettes put to sea in 1940 the crews were keen but totally lacking in knowledge of the sea, let alone experience in anti-submarine warfare. In the RN the comparable corvettes invariably carried a solid cadre of veterans in key positions, but in the RCN most of the veterans were shifted ashore at the commencement of hostilities to training positions. The commanding officers, mostly reservists drawn from the merchant marine, were as a rule the only men aboard with substantial previous sea time, and the crews, who a few months earlier might have been rounding up cattle in Alberta, had little chance to learn their jobs before being hurled into battle against the Kriegsmarine's well-trained U-boat fleet.

The escort group commanders were very young by Royal Navy standards, pitchforked into assuming heavy responsibilities in their late twenties, backed up by four or five rag-tag corvettes designated as the escort group. Besides lacking proper working up as individual units, the corvettes had even less practice at operating together as a group, and their crews had little intuitive grasp of the likely intentions of their escort commander in any given situation. But desperate circumstances demanded desperate remedies; at a critical juncture of the Battle of the Atlantic, as the only escorts available to Canada, they proved to be a bulwark against the annihilation of the merchantmen in their charge.

The grimmest losses occurred in the slow convoys, which were for the most part left to the care of the Canadian corvettes, and postwar analysis confirmed what was sensed at the time, namely that slow ships were three times more likely to fall victim to a torpedo than their speedier sisters. It is not surprising therefore that convoys like SC42 in 1941 took a murderous drubbing, and reached the Western Approaches having lost a quarter of their ships.

These early Canadian ships were fitted with an obsolete type of asdic, no gyro compass, no radar, and secondary armament consisting of whatever odds and ends could be found. Moreover, they lacked the professional calibre of shore support available to British boats, and stood at the bottom of the list when it came to maintenance and resupply from the Canadian bases. As time passed, better radar and more efficient weaponry were fitted, and in the end most Canadian corvettes were modified in a similar way to their RN sisters. For the most part, however, these changes came later than in the comparable RN ships, and Canada's Flowers had their finest hour before such refinements had been implemented. Some understanding of the desperate hardships endured at sea and the dodges, including bribery of dockyard personnel, used to bring the ships up to fighting efficiency can be gained from the books by Lamb and Easton noted above.

By 1945 the RCN had 400 ships, manned by well trained and battle-hardened crews. Canadian escort groups had taken over the major responsibility for North Atlantic convoys and had become very good indeed at their job. In 1939 Canada had had a permanent naval force of fewer than 2000 men, whereas at the war's end she had the third largest Allied navy, expanded by a factor of 50 to 100,000 men. By comparison, the personnel strength of the Royal Navy had expanded by a factor of 8.

Evolution of the Flower class

During World War I Smith's Dock Limited of South Bank, Middlesbrough, had built a class of anti-submarine patrol boat known as the Z-boats, the design of which owed something to the prewar steam whaler. Early in 1939 the same firm made a proposal to the Admiralty for the construction of a 'patrol vessel of the whaler type', envisaged as an escort for coastal convoys. This is commonly claimed to have been based on the design of their whaler *Southern Pride* (see *Selected Papers on British Warship Design in World War II*, Elliott's *Allied Escort Ships of World War II*, Lynch's *Canada's Flowers: A History of the Corvettes of Canada*, Preston and Raven's *Flower Class Corvettes*, Costello and Hughes' *The Battle of the Atlantic*, and German's *The Sea is at our Gates*). Where this vessel actually stood in relation to the average steam whaleboat (Norwegian *hvalbåt*, German *Walfangboot*) of the mid-1930s is therefore worth a short comment.

In 1935 a small consortium of Norwegian whaling companies ordered from Fredriksstad Mekanisk Verksted a vessel named *H J Bull* (Norwegian pronunciation is approximately Ha-Yott-Bill), an 'observation catcher' of radical design. Bigger, faster and with larger bunkers than her contemporaries, she was designed to range out from the factory ship, note where the best hunting opportunities existed, and coordinate the activities of the expedition's other catcher boats. Three more such 'scout catchers' were built in the run-up to the War: *Southern Pride* by Smith's Dock in 1936, and *Southern Gem* and *Unitas I* by Bremer Vulkan in Germany the following year. All four bunkered 400 tons of oil, double the capacity of the average prewar whaler, and had an overall length of just over 170ft, some 30ft longer (see Sketch A).

Arrangement drawings of *Southern Pride* are not available, but Sketch

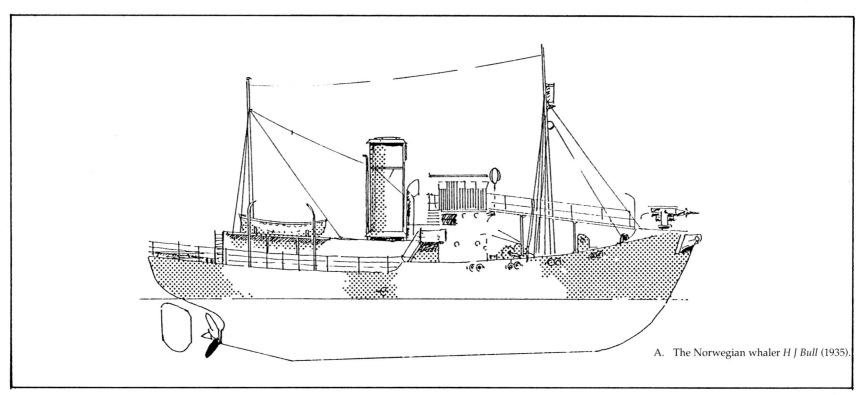

A. The Norwegian whaler *H J Bull* (1935).

B. The whaler *Southern Pride* (1936).

B, based on several plan fragments, drawings of the other three scout catchers and several somewhat unsatisfactory photographs, gives an indication of her profile. Like the other scout catchers, she differed from the average whaler in having an extra long casing, with the lifeboats shifted well aft to leave the side fuel hatches clear. The profile of the stern was unlike that of the later corvettes in two particulars: the counter was of rounded canoe shape, without a knuckle, and the curved line linking the propeller boss to the keel was unique to *Pride*, resembling neither the joggled configuration of the corvette nor the straight line found in other whalers.

While there is no doubt of the whaleboat ancestry of the corvette's hull form, in my view the specific importance of *Southern Pride* has perhaps been exaggerated. *Pride* was, after all, only one of 125 whalers turned out by the Middlesbrough yard between the wars, and we must take into account the expertise gained by chief designer William Reed in designing anti-submarine vessels in World War I. I have examined this question more fully in 'The Design of the Flower class Corvette and its Relationship to the Whaler *Southern Pride* of 1936' in *Warship 1991*).

Gladiolus, the very first 'Patrol Vessel of Whaler Type', was launched at Middlesbrough in January 1940. Thirty-five feet longer than *Southern Pride*, she did not, at first glance, particularly resemble a whaleboat. She had much less pronounced sheer, and the above water profile suggested if anything an armed trawler with its short forecastle and an enclosed compass house rather than the open 'hunting bridge' and exposed steering position of the steam whaler. The funnel and masts had a slight rake, despite the fact that Smith's Dock whalers were distinguished from those of other builders, such as Kaldenes, by their vertical funnels. Sketch C shows the slightly later corvette *Periwinkle* as commissioned (the class underwent a great many changes as the war progressed, and later versions differed greatly from *Gladiolus* and her immediate successors).

Nonetheless, the corvette's hull lines, particularly the cut-up at the after end of the keel, rounded forefoot, cruiser stern and spade rudder, were thoroughly characteristic of the whaler prototype. This stern configuration had been pioneered by Smith's Dock with *Southern Spray* in 1925, and by 1930 had been adopted by all other whaleboat builders in Germany and Norway. Trawler builders also adopted the cruiser stern in the late 1930s, but retained the classic type of stern frame and 'barn door' rudder. By 1939, with the exceptions of the RN *Basset* class and the RCN *Fundy* class trawlers, the spade rudder was the point of distinction between the stern of a whalecatcher and that of a trawler.

The drawings in this book are based on the plans used at the Burrard Dry Dock Company's yard in Vancouver, and closely follow the original drawings from Middlesbrough apart from the squared-off stern and the shortened casing. The semaphore machine shown was fitted in some of the first Canadian corvettes, as was the ¾in mild steel 'conning tower' or

C. The corvette *Periwinkle*.

machine gun screen shown on the starboard side, just abaft the compass house. This had been fitted as a 'dodger' on the early British corvettes, to give the men on the bridge some protection against light-calibre machine gun fire, to which escorts were exposed when strafed by low-flying enemy aircraft (a particular hazard for convoys on the British East Coast). The helmsman's back was protected by a similar box-like screen installed in the wheelhouse. These were later removed.

Though the aptness of the word 'corvette' may be questioned on historical grounds, and despite uncertainty as to exactly whose inspiraton it was to designate the new vessels as such, the word has certain romantic connotations not shared by the phrase 'Patrol Vessel of Whaler Type'. The Flower names given to the British corvettes followed a tradition started by the Herbaceous Border sloops of World War I, while the subsequent Castle class were named for British castles. The corvettes of the RCN, on the other hand, were named for towns in Canada; *Agassiz* is a farming community in the fertile Fraser Valley in British Columbia. Ten Canadian-built corvettes originally intended for the Royal Navy but subsequently manned by the RCN (though remaining under RN operational control and based in UK rather than Canadian waters) retained their Flower names.

In Britain, the last Flower was commissioned in 1943, reflecting the Admiralty's brisk recognition that the corvette was simply too small for mid-ocean duty in the Atlantic and the construction of longer vessels better suited to this task, notably the 250ft Castle class corvette and the 300ft twin-screw frigates (a comparison of the relative sizes of the whaler *Southern Gem*, a Flower class corvette and a Castle class corvette is shown in Sketch D). However, the smaller Canadian yards such as those at Collingwood and Kingston continued to build corvettes until 1944. One reason for this was the limitation on size imposed by the locks on the canals through which the ships had to pass on their way from the Great Lakes to the Saint Lawrence River.

Operational history of HMCS *Agassiz*

HMCS *Agassiz* was laid down at the yard of the Burrard Dry Dock Company, Vancouver, on 23 April 1940, launched on 15 August and commissioned on 23 January 1941 with Lt B D L Johnson RCNR in command. In March, with sisterships *Westaskiwin* and *Alberni*, she sailed for Halifax, Nova Scotia, via the Panama Canal. Joining the Newfoundland Escort Force in May, she was immediately employed escorting Atlantic convoys. In September, escorting the hard-pressed SC 44, she picked up many of the survivors from the corvette *Levis*, which had been torpedoed by U74 (Kapt Lt E F Kentrat).

In June 1942, accompanying ONS 102 as part of Escort Group A 3 (led by Cdr Heinemann USN), she helped to drive off a series of U-boat attacks in which U94 and U590 were damaged by depth charges.

Her most exciting passage was with ON 115 in July 1942, as part of

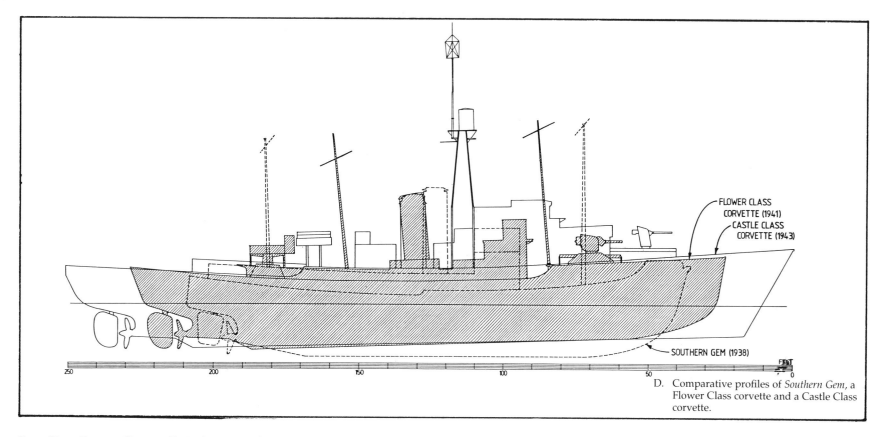

D. Comparative profiles of *Southern Gem*, a Flower Class corvette and a Castle Class corvette.

Canadian Escort Group C 3 (commanded by Cdr D C Wallace in *Saguenay*). This complicated convoy battle, during which U588 was sunk after a skilful and persistent attack by *Skeena* and *Westaskiwin*, is fully described in Marc Milner's *North Atlantic Run*. During the battle, *Agassiz* opened fire on a surfaced U-boat, and picked up survivors from the torpedoed Royal Mail steamer *Lochkatrine*. Later she took the crippled tanker *G S Waldron* in tow, an action for which her crew were subsequently paid salvage money.

In August 1942 she escorted convoy TAW 12, which lost several ships to determined attacks by U600 (Kapt Lt Zermühlen) and U598 (Kapt Lt Holtorf). (A note about the designation letters for Atlantic convoys may be useful here: SC convoys were eastbound from Sydney, Nova Scotia, to the United Kingdom, while 'outward' ON and ONS – S indicating 'slow' – convoys returned in the opposite direction; TAW stood for Trinidad-Aruba-Key West.)

On 4 January 1943 she began a major refit at Liverpool, Nova Scotia, and in April, now commanded by Lt Cdr E M Moore RCNR, joined the newly formed Escort Group C 1. From December 1943 to March 1944 she underwent a major refit at Staten Island, New York, which included the lengthening of her forecastle, and subsequently joined Escort Group W 2 of the Western Escort Force. In August she was transferred to W 7, and was employed mainly on coastal escort duties until the end of hostilities.

HMCS *Agassiz* paid off on 14 June 1945 at Sydney, Nova Scotia, and she was broken up in the course of the following year.

Modifications

The first corvettes had two masts. The foremast was placed forward of the bridge, where it tended to interfere with the view from the compass platform and shower the men on the bridge with precipitated moisture (the position of the masts was determined by the need for a long radio antenna in ships working on the Northern Patrol between the Faeroes and Iceland). Later the foremast was shifted abaft the bridge, and the mainmast removed.

The presence of the mainmast abaft the engine room skylight in the first Canadian corvettes explains the difference in position of the 2pdr between the early British and Canadian corvettes. To avoid interference with the field of fire of the 2pdr, the gun was shifted to the after end of the casing in Canadian vessels, and remained there even after the mast had been deleted.

The early corvettes turned out to be extremely wet ships; a sea shipped over the forecastle roared aft unimpeded to smack down on to the deck just forward of the bridge. This problem was alleviated in the later versions by the provision of greater sheer and flare to the hull form forward and breakwaters abaft the anchor windlass and forward of the wheelhouse, and, most significantly, by the extension of the forecastle back to a point abreast the funnel. Corvettes were not the only vessels to have their seaworthiness improved by lengthening the forecastle in this way; similar modifications were made to the Dance class and RNZN *Kiwi* class trawlers. Other notable modifications included the provision of anti-splinter armour plates abreast the 4in gun forward and the 2pdr aft.

In 1940, because of the shortage of fleet minesweepers, a number of corvettes were equipped for this duty. Twenty-four British and fifty-four Canadian corvettes, including *Agassiz*, were fitted for sweeping contact mines using Oropesa gear (details of this equipment will be found below). To improve the minesweeping capabilities of the RCN ships, the stern was squared off to make room for the sweep rollers and the engine room casing was shortened by 8ft (from frame 89 to frame 93) to give more room on the sweep deck and to accommodate the minesweeping winch. Shortening the casing necessitated the repositioning of the galley forward to just abaft the bridge. The early corvettes tended to trim by the head when fully loaded, and this interfered with the working of the asdic; it was resolved to some extent by the addition of extra weight aft. The ten ships sent incomplete to Britain (those retaining Flower names) were not modified in this fashion.

Hull form and construction

For hunting whales the catcher had to be quick off the mark and capable of making rapid twists and turns; these requirements were no less important in anti-submarine warfare. Directional stability was less important than agility, and this was reflected in the cutting away of the fin areas at bow and stern, allowing the extremities to slide sideways briskly in a turn. The corvette's rise of floor was rather less than that of the average whaler, but it had the same generous radius at the bilge to accommodate the Scotch boiler and side fuel tanks, giving the hull a rather tubby look amidships.

The block coefficient, or ratio of the volume of the underwater portion of the hull to a rectangular block defined by the same hull's length, breadth and draught, varies with the actual draught. The more 'rounded off' the midship section, and the more the fore and after bodies are cut away, the finer the hull lines. In a very general way, the magnitude of the coefficient corresponds directly to cargo-carrying capacity, and inversely to speed. Figures for the block coefficient of the corvette are not available, but those of *H J Bull* were 0.47 light and 0.56 at all up displacement.

The whaler's hull was specially strengthened for work in the ice by the generous use of fore-and-aft stringers and by placing the forward frames closer together than those aft. The frames in the corvettes were of angle iron, spaced a uniform 22in apart, and a plate keel was used rather than the whaler's bar keel. There was a structural weakness abreast the engine room because of the absence of deck beams and, as in many whalers, the corvette hull was fitted with four frames with reverses at this point, reinforced by a stringer. The shell consisted of six 'in and out' strakes, and different yards used different methods of dealing with the resulting space between the 'out' strakes and the frames: Smith's Dock used joggled plates, while other builders used packing pieces or joggled frames. Burrard, who built *Agassiz*, joggled the plates.

Bilge keels were rarely used in whalecatchers because of the danger that they might cut the whale-line when the boat had a 'fast fish'. In corvettes substantial bilge keels almost a foot across were initially fitted, and these were subsequently increased to an impressive 22in in an attempt to ameliorate rolling.

Superstructure

At the upper deck level were the commanding officer's cabin to starboard and the officers' washroom to port. In whalecatchers, to allow unimpeded communication between the bridge, crow's nest and gunner, the hunting bridge and the steering position were always open to the weather, but the 'Patrol Vessel of Whaler Type' was designed with a closed wheelhouse similar to that in a trawler, with a closed compass house/chartroom/asdic room above, thus producing a superstructure with three levels.

Some ships quickly contrived a small 'bridge' above the compass house, which gave the officer of the watch a better view, particularly when the platform for the 4in gun was raised somewhat from its original level. Later, the compass house was replaced by an open compass platform which was extended forward by a house containing the asdic apparatus and the chartroom, and extended laterally by wings on which twin machine guns, and later 20mm cannon, were fitted. Photographs show considerable variation in the exact pattern of struts supporting these bridge wing extensions.

In five years of wartime service and in 270 vessels, photographic evidence shows considerable variation on the original layout of the superstructure. When the Canadian short-forecastle corvettes had the forecastle extended aft, enclosing the commanding officer's cabin below deck, the wheelhouse now sat almost at deck level, with the galley and commanding officer's cabin protruding above deck by 2ft 9in and 2ft respectively, and the galley roof forming a sort of platform just abaft the wheelhouse.

In the Modified Flower class the commanding officer's cabin was again shifted to upper deck level, with the wheelhouse and radio office above it and the compass platform above these, again giving a three-level configuration; this arrangement is also found in ten units of the Canadian Revised class corvettes and a few other British examples.

In prewar days the position of the galley was one of the features which distinguished a whaler from a trawler; in the former it was always amidships, and in the latter invariably at the after end of the casing. In the original Middlesbrough proposal the galley was installed trawler fashion, in the after casing on the port side. In the Canadian corvettes the galley was shifted forward just abaft the bridge and above the forward boiler room. Because of the height of the Scotch boiler, this meant that the galley deck was somewhat higher than that of the CO's cabin, and this was reflected in a joggle in the profile of the casing. Initially the galley stovepipe ran up abaft the bridge, but it was subsequently angled back to run up forward of the funnel. The galley stove was kerosene (paraffin) fired, and the Canadian ships had a small refrigerator. In some later British-built vessels the galley was enclosed in a house at upper deck level, and in fact some British corvettes actually had two galleys. The model of the Norwegian corvette *Andenes* (ex-*Acanthus*) on display at Horten shows this arrangement.

Accommodation

For coastal escort duties a crew of twenty-nine had been contemplated, but this was clearly inadequate for mid-ocean service, and to man the additional armament and other equipment subsequently added. The complement ultimately reached eighty-five, though living space and facilities did not increase in proportion. In the Modified Flowers the complement was even higher: up to 109 men. The living spaces were steam heated, but the first British corvettes used coal-fired bogie stoves.

Machinery and bunkers

The four scout catchers were exceptions to the rule that prewar whalers were powered by three-cylinder triple expansion engines. The *H J Bull* had a double compound Fredriksstad Steam Motor, and the other three were powered by four-cylinder triples (each with two low pressure cylinders). The engine in *Southern Pride* developed 2300ihp, and those in the German-built catchers 2400ihp. Since the casting patterns for the Pride's engine were available, they were used for the corvette's engine in preference to designing a new engine from scratch. By slightly enlarging the diameter of the HP cylinder and increasing the revolutions to 185rpm, the designers produced a naval version which could develop 2750ihp.

Reversing gear was of the Stephenson 'all-round' type, shifting from ahead to astern whichever way it was turned. In the frigates a direct-acting 'push' type reversing engine was used.

This relatively simple powerplant was chosen because it was familiar to the engineers of the day and could be produced in relatively unsophisticated engine shops. Rather than using encased working parts and forced lubrication, the design was entirely open, with crankshafts and crossheads in full view, to facilitate repairs. Bearing temperature was monitored by feel, and lubrication was manual in the first engines, though Manzell lubricators were later fitted. This open design, with a stroke of only 30in and without forced lubrication had the disadvantage that engine speeds above 185rpm were not possible.

An engine of almost identical design, with a slightly modified cylinder entablature and the condenser shifted to the opposite side, was fitted in the Bay and River class twin-screw frigates, the American *Tacoma* class patrol frigates and in the British Landing Ship Tank (3), beside the Castle class corvette. The provision of a coupling at both ends of the engine allowed the decision on which side of the frigate it should be installed to be postponed until a relatively late stage in the ship's construction. The Castles were powered by what was in effect the starboard engine of a frigate. In the end, an astonishing total of some 1150 of these engines were built – a truly remarkable record for a machine which had started life as the engine of a humble whaler (this total is given in *Selected Papers on British Warship Design in World War II*; we have had some difficulty in confirming the exact total). A 1/10 scale model of the engine can be seen at the Museum of Science & Engineering at Newcastle-upon-Tyne. The difference in speed between *Southern Pride* (15.25 knots), the Flowers (16 knots) and the Castles (16.5 knots), all using the same engine, is a neat demonstration of the relationship between waterline length and speed. The engine photograph in this book shows an engine ready for installation in *Drumheller*, one of the Collingwood corvettes.

Postwar whalers were, for the most part, fitted with a pair of D-type watertube boilers, placed side by side. Apart from the watertube boilers installed in a few boats by Kaldnes of Tønsberg and Smith's Dock of Middlesbrough in the late 1930s, however, prewar whalecatchers were usually outfitted with a single Scotch firetube boiler. The scout catchers *H J Bull*, *Southern Gem* and *Unitas I* had two Scotch boilers, placed back to back, but *Southern Pride* was unique, with one firetube and one watertube boiler. The first was used alone for economical cruising.

William Reed had originally planned to use watertube boilers in the corvette; in the event, however, the more sophisticated type were urgently needed for more important classes of warship, so the first corvettes were fitted with a pair of three-furnace Scotch boilers of classic whaleboat type. These were fitted in separate boiler rooms, and the heating surface totalled 7150sq ft. Closed ashpit forced draught of the traditional Howden type was used, air being forced into the furnace by a 36in Sirocco fan. Some of the Belfast-built corvettes were fitted with the slightly more sophisticated Howden-Johnson boilers. The Modified Flower class used forced draught of the closed stokehold type (that is to say, the fireroom had airtight doors and was kept at a higher pressure than the ambient air by powerful fans).

Whalers working in the Antarctic started using oil fuel in 1925 and, with rare exceptions, all those in service in 1939 were oil-fired. The average sized whaler carried about 200 tons in four tanks placed athwartships below the bridge. The scout catchers' bunker capacity was doubled to about 400 tons, with most of the additional fuel carried in side tanks abreast the boiler rooms. Trawlers of a similar size and date invariably burnt coal, carried in an athwartship bunker under the bridge; they also carried coal in the fish room which they burnt on the outward passage to the fishing grounds. Coal firing was considered as an alternative for the corvettes, but in the end it was decided to follow whaler practice. Because the vessels were intended for use in coastal operations, bunker capacity of 230 tons was judged adequate, carried in side tanks; this gave a range of 5000 miles at economical cruising speed of 10 knots. The space corresponding to the athwartship bunker in a whaler was used as accommodation. In the first year of corvette operations bunkering at sea was not practised, and an escort running out of fuel had to be towed to port; by late 1941, however, corvettes began refuelling from tankers in the convoys.

The Modified corvettes (or 'Corvettes with Increased Endurance' as the RCN called them) bunkered 300 tons, and could manage 7400 miles at 10 knots. The extra capacity was obtained by increasing the size of the tanks under the messdeck and those abreast the boiler rooms, which was possible because the watertube boilers were much smaller and lighter than the Scotch type originally fitted. Each Scotch boiler contained 27 tons of water, and in fact it was necessary to ballast the later corvettes because the watertube boilers weighed so much less. A scrap merchant in Kingston, Ontario, breaking up a corvette just after the war, had an unexpected windfall when he found that his purchase had been ballasted with 70 tons of valuable pig lead.

Although it was not a practical consideration during the war, corvettes converted to whalecatchers were found (according to Kapt Hans Garling, Kapt Helmut Tiemayer and Kapt Sven Thienemann) to handle sluggishly with full bunkers, and consequently only topped up their tanks on the way to and from the hunting grounds. If we assume that the displacement of a converted corvette was about 1000 tons, an extra 100 tons of oil might be expected to increase the vessel's weight by about 10 percent. The first corvettes displaced about 950 tons, and the Modifieds just over 1000 tons. (The conversions, being merchant ships, were registered at 700 tons gross, which is actually a measure of enclosed volume rather than weight.)

The whaler propeller was a four-bladed casting of steel or stainless steel. The choice of metal is explained because bronze became brittle in Antarctic water temperatures. *Southern Pride*'s screw was 11ft in diameter, 10ft 3in in pitch, and had an area of 47sq ft; this was typical for a whaler. For the corvette the naval constructors chose a three-bladed bronze propeller, 10ft 6in in diameter, 10ft 8in in pitch and 31sq ft in area,

Steering gear

Steam steering was used in whalers from about 1910, much earlier than in trawlers of the same size. Initially the steering engine was installed on the bridge, and used only when hunting. Later it was shifted back to the after end of the casing. In both cases it was connected to the rudder quadrant by rods and chains. In whalers from *H J Bull* (1935) onwards the casing was extended further aft, almost to the counter, allowing the use of a steam steering engine placed almost on top of the rudder head and employing the Wilson-Pirrie 'loose quadrant/fixed tiller' system. The tiller, solidly connected to the rudder stock, was connected by a pair of heavy springs to the quadrant, which was turned by the steering engine. This arrangement prevented damage to the steering engine by backlash if the rudder was struck by heavy cross seas. In the corvettes, because of the necessity of fitting depth charge rails and other equipment on the quarterdeck, this plan was modified, and the steering engine and emergency wheel were fitted below the main deck, in a compartment right at the stern.

Anchor windlass

Sackville's winch shown in the photograph in this book was built by Clarke Chapman Ltd, and we believe this was fitted after the war. The original winch would, however, also have been of classic merchant service pattern and virtually identical. Steam drove a pair of horizontal cylinders, with the cranks arranged at 90 degrees to each other so that one or the other would always start. A simple reversing valve was used rather than gear of the Stephenson type. The warping drums rotated when the crankshaft turned, and the cable gypsy could be engaged and disengaged with a dog clutch. The band brakes were controlled by a simple screw arrangement.

Armament

The primary armament of the corvette was a 4in gun forward and a single 2pdr pom-pom on a bandstand aft, both of World War I vintage. The early corvettes all used the Mark IX breech-loading gun with its box-like shield, while the Modifieds were fitted with the Mark XIX 4in QF gun on a HA/LA mounting and a smaller shield. The term 'breech-loading' originally differentiated a modern gun from the muzzle-loaders which had disappeared in the course of the 19th century, but at this date it indicated only that the projectile was loaded first, followed by a bag containing the powder. The QF version used 'fixed' ammunition, with the projectile secured to the shell casing containing the propellant. Ten partially-completed Canadian corvettes with Flower names crossed the Atlantic on their way to fitting out in the UK armed only with wooden cannon, a deceptive measure which was by all accounts singularly unconvincing.

Later, in those ships which were involved in the D-Day landings, four extra 20mm Oerlikons were installed on the engine room casing as a precaution against air attack; in the early days, however, the corvettes were outfitted with whatever odds and ends happened to be available, such as twin Browning 0.5in or Lewis 0.303in machine guns. These were sited on the extended bridge wings, as were projectors for PAC rockets (the parachute-and-cable device was more useful as a morale booster than as a useful defence against strafing aircraft). For details of these weapons, and others such as the 6pdr Hotchkiss Mark II gun occasionally found on corvettes, see the first-rate drawings by John Lambert in John Campbell's *Naval Weapons of World War II*.

Snowflake rocket flares were later used instead of starshells to light up a surfaced U-boat at night, and launchers for these were fitted at each side of the 4in gun shield.

British weapons were classified either by calibre or by weight of projectile. The projectile fired by the corvette's 4in gun weighed about 31lb. The 40mm '2pdr' projectile actually weighed about 1.7lb, substantially lighter than that of the Bofors 40mm. The 20mm Oerlikon projectile weighed just over ¼lb. The 6pdr Hotchkiss fitted in a few corvettes had a calibre of 57mm. It is worth noting that the 2pdr to be seen aboard the preserved HMCS *Sackville* was salvaged from an Irish Navy corvette.

Depth charges carried on the corvettes were basically identical to those developed during World War I. The Mark VII was a cylinder 28in long and 18in in diameter containing 300lb of explosive, the whole weighing about 420lb. A tube ran through its centre, and at opposite ends of this were the primer and pistol, which could be set to explode at a predetermined depth. Securing a 150lb weight to the charge increased its rate of descent: charges so weighted formed the 'heavy' part of the pattern. A pattern consisted of a minimum of five charges, but later ten or more were used. The charges were dropped from rails at the stern or launched laterally by throwers. The pair of single rails used in the early corvettes was later modified to allow a double tier of charges.

The impact of the explosive charge in the chamber of the Mark I depth charge thrower fitted in the early corvettes hurled the charge and the 'stalk' or carrier to which it was secured about 40 yards. The thrower was cocked with a spring-loaded handle and fired with a lanyard which pulled out the pin holding the arrangement in the cocked position. Corvettes initially had two, and later four, throwers and the depth charges and carriers were stowed along the casing. In the more sophisticated Mark IV thrower, this arrangement was modified so that the carrier or arbor acted only as a piston, and was retained for re-use. Examples of this more sophisticated version, with their conspicuous recoil cylinders, can be seen on board HMCS *Sackville*.

The numbers of depth charges carried increased with time. Some early boats were fitted with as few as twenty-five, while the Modified corvettes carried up to one hundred. In the corvettes fitted for LL or Oropesa sweeping there were greater space and weight constraints on the number of depth charges.

Depth charges exploded astern of the corvette, and the attacking vessel lost asdic contact as she approached and ran over the U-boat. The exact position of the U-boat as the corvette passed over it therefore had to be guessed, and the U-boat commanders became skilled at using this loss of contact as an opportunity to take evasive action. An anti-submarine weapon which could throw ahead, and thus cut down this dead time, was therefore required. Corvettes were too lightly built to mount the most powerful ahead-throwing weapon, the Squid, but they were fitted with another very effective type known as a Hedgehog.

This consisted of twenty-four spigots, each of which carried a bomb about 20in long, containing 30lb of explosive and weighing about 60lb in total. The bomb was propelled by a charge in the base, fired electrically. While the corvette maintained asdic contact, the bombs could be hurled up to 400 yards ahead of the ship, and the only time in which the U-boat could take evasive action was the few seconds the bombs were in the air. A 'ripple switch' fired the bombs asynchronously, and the spigots were arranged so that the bombs fell in a narrow figure-of-eight pattern. In the corvette the hedgehog was placed abaft and on the starboard side of the 4in gun, its weight balanced by the bombs in a ready-use locker on the port side.

Hedgehog bombs exploded on contact, rather than at a preset depth, so an explosion indicated an actual hit. Consequently, an unsuccessful attack had much less of a psychological effect on the quarry than did a near miss by a depth charge. Depth charges were in any event preferred if asdic contact was not solid.

Minesweeping equipment

Oropesa sweeping for contact mines was a system developed during World War I aboard the armed trawler *Oropesa* (hence the name). Contact mines floated at a set distance below the surface, secured by a mooring wire to an anchor on the seabed. Cutting the mooring line caused the mine to pop to the surface, where it could be sunk by gunfire.

The sweep wire was laid up with one strand running the wrong way, so that it acted like a neurosurgeon's Gigli saw, rasping its way through the mooring wire. To aid this action, the wire could also be fitted with wire cutters. In theory the mine was supposed to disarm itself when the cable was cut, but in fact the hulls of the sweepers were constantly exposed to explosions from mines which had failed to demonstrate good manners in this respect.

The torpedo-shaped float to which the sweep wire was attached was dragged out laterally on the sweeping vessel's quarter by a multiplane 'otter', and held at the correct depth by another multiplane, the 'kite' (otter and kite were identical; the difference in action depended on how they were rigged). This gear was swung in and out by a pair of heavy davits which are conspicuous in photographs.

Information on the minesweeping winch used in corvettes is scarce, so the details given below are not definitive. The illustration included in the Drawings section of this book represents a 'best guess', based on fragmentary sources and the odd snapshot.

There was some variation between winch manufacturers, but all winches featured two large drums for the float wires and a central smaller one for the kite wire. Reversing gear was not really needed since the sweep ran out under its own weight, but it seems that most installations incorporated a reversing valve. The warping heads were keyed to the shaft and rotated when the engine was turning, but the three wire drums could be clutched independently, each having its own band brake operated by a wheel. In the case of the outer drums, a dial indicated how much wire had run out, and an automatic spooling guide ensured that the wire fed on smoothly when heaving in. This was disconnected when streaming the float.

Power was supplied by a two-cylinder engine, with the cylinders configured in a variety of ways. In British minesweeping corvettes and *Albury* class sweepers, they were placed on either side as in the trawl winch which was the machine's direct ancestor. In the Canadian (Stevens-Adamson) winch, they were placed side by side just forward of the winch on the port side, with the piston rods fore and aft, as shown in the illustration in this book. In the case of the winches fitted in the British *Algerine* and Australian *Bathurst* class sweepers, the engine was located as in the Canadian version, but the cylinders lay athwartship and the crankshaft was connected to the winch via bevel gears.

We were able to obtain a drawing of the type of winch fitted in the *Bathurst* class through the kindness of Commodore (E) Tom Fisher RAN. Four pinions drove four large gear wheels (one turning the second motion shaft and warping heads), while vertical levers controlling dog clutches engaged and declutched the three wire drums. Three compound adjustable band-brakes were controlled by horizontal wheels; a spring held each band clear of the brake drum when disengaged. In the *Bathurst* class (though not in the corvettes) spare sweep wire was stored on a large reel below deck, which was turned using a power take-off from the winch above it and clutched and disengaged using a lever just inside the port warping head. Herringbone gears can be heavily loaded, and were used rather than simple spur gears (although they complicated slightly the operation of the dog clutch, since the pinion could not simply slide in and out as it did on the similarly-sized whale winch found on catchers. Some Canadian *Bangors* used a winch built by an American manufacturer of logging winches; this was possibly also used in some corvettes built on the West Coast, and according to Admiral Tony Storrs it functioned very well.

Ideally, Oropesa gear was handled on a roomy 'sweep deck' as found in the British *Algerines*, but in other vessels it was crammed into whatever space was available. In the case of the British corvettes the basic hull shape and superstructure were unchanged, and room was made by reducing the number of depth charges carried to ten. Since these vessels lacked the squared off stern and shortened casing of their Canadian counterparts, there cannot have been much room.

The minefield was swept in a series of passes, with the sweepers in echelon, each ship travelling in the safe strip swept by the ship ahead. The area cleared was marked by Dan buoys, a task undertaken in the minesweeping flotillas by specially fitted Dan laying trawlers. In Canadian corvettes the buoys were stowed on the casing aft, a portable gallows being fitted on each side to handle them.

Acoustic mines were actuated by the noise of a ship's propeller; the countermeasure was simply to produce sufficient noise to detonate the mine well ahead of the ship. In the case of the sixteen British corvettes fitted for magnetic and acoustic sweeping, this was achieved using a bucket containing an electrically-driven Kango hammer fitted on a retractable A-frame at the bow (the first such devices were made by Kango Ltd, who made jackhammers in peacetime). The A-frame at the bow added considerably to the difficulty of bringing a corvette alongside; Lt Cdr Tom Hand RNR, first commanding officer of *Bryony*, recalls that he persuaded the Admiralty to let him remove the A-frame after he had snagged it under a dockside crane and almost pried the crane loose from its mooring on the quay. The A-frame was replaced by an acoustic hammer lowered on an athwartship boom.

Magnetic mines were laid on the bottom in shallow water and detonated by the influence of a ship's magnetic field as it passed overhead. A 'degaussing' cable minimised the magnetic field of the minesweeping vessel; a conspicuous feature of the earliest British corvettes was the way in which this degaussing cable was run outside the hull plating, but it was soon shifted inside the bulwarks. The mine on the sea floor could be detonated by a powerful magnetic field produced some distance astern of the sweeper. This field was generated by pulsing a current through electrodes trailed astern of the sweeper on buoyant cables.

In minesweeping whalers and trawlers, streaming and recovering the sweep meant that the LL cable had to be manhandled over the stern. 'In sweep' was an all-hands job, with the cable dragged aboard and stowed in bights on either side of the casing. The earliest British corvettes fitted for magnetic/acoustic sweeping followed the same practice, but in later boats the LL cables were stowed on a large reel just abaft the casing; this fitting took up the same space as an Oropesa minesweeping winch. Various schemes were tried. First, room had to be found for extra specialist personnel, besides space for the generator and batteries. These last were installed in the after accommodation space originally intended for the petty officers, and the need for extra accommodation forward was a further reason for extending the forecastle; *Bryony* was in fact enclosed almost to the after end of the casing, though this configuration was not repeated in any other Flower. In *Gloxinia* the casing was widened 18in on either side and the generators were installed on a sort of shelf in the engine room. Photographs of *Peony* and *Gloxinia* taken in the Mediterranean in about 1943 show structural additions, presumably 'sweeping messes', abaft the bridge. In purpose-built sweepers, since the bow was the most vulnerable part of the ship, the forward messdecks were cleared while sweeping, and the hands were accommodated in temporary living space in the after part of the vessel.

Asdic and radar

The first RCN corvettes had no gyro compasses and were fitted with an obsolete type of asdic, the British Type 123A. The compass, graduated in points rather than degrees, and the wheel lock for rotating the asdic dome were in the compass house. The equipment was later shifted into a compartment forward of the compass platform. The formidable technical obstacles confronting the commanding officer of an RCN corvette attacking a U-boat with this primitive equipment are well described in Marc Milner's *The North Atlantic Run*.

The acronym 'radar' was of American origin. In the first four years of the war the equipment was referred to as 'RDF' (Radio Direction Finding). A conspicuous feature of the later corvettes was the Perspex lantern protecting the 'cheese' antennae of the Type 271 radar; in earlier versions this lantern was of wood with glass panels, usually hidden under a canvas cover when the vessel was in harbour. The equipment was capable of picking up a U-boat on the surface, and was positioned to one side of the vessel to avoid back echoes from the funnel and mast. Because of its weight, it could not be mounted at the masthead like the American SL radar, which fulfilled the same function, and its range suffered accordingly. Some who served in vessels fitted with this type of radar were, however, very impressed with its performance.

Many photographs show Canadian corvettes sporting a fishbone aerial resembling the postwar UHF television Yagi antenna. One version of this was the SW2CQ ('Swick'), a gadget invented in Canada and used until sufficient 271 sets were available: it was rotated by a car steering wheel connected by bicycle chain to a ramshackle arrangement of tubing which ran up the mast.

The 'flying bedspring' antenna of the British Type 286 radar, fitted in a few British corvettes, did not rotate fully but was able to detect a surfaced U-boat ahead.

Type 291 was an air-warning radar fitted in some corvettes. The antenna was X shaped, with a horizontal H at each extremity. As it was light, it could be mounted at the masthead; later models were motor-driven.

For wolf pack U-boat tactics to succeed, individual U-boats had to send sighting reports by radio to U-boat command. The 'birdcage' HF/DF (High Frequency Direction Finding) antenna fitted at the mastheads of many escorts, including Castle class corvettes, could pinpoint a U-boat ahead of the convoy the moment it began transmitting to Brest. Running out on that bearing, firing starshells and dropping depth charges, the escort could at the very least force the U-boat to dive, and with luck make a successful attack on it. This extremely useful device was not fitted to the Flowers because they lacked the speed to make effective use of it.

The antenna for the Type 244 was often mounted on top of the Type 271 lantern. It consisted of four 'egg-timer' aerials, and was the interrogator of the IFF (Identify Friend or Foe) radar. A second egg-timer antenna (Type 253) fixed to a spur on the mast or other suitable place, was the responder, returning the appropriate reassuring pulse when picked up by the interrogator of another friendly vessel.

For navigational purposes, corvettes were fitted with a medium frequency direction finder of the type used in merchantmen. The antennae consisted of two circular elements at right angles to each other.

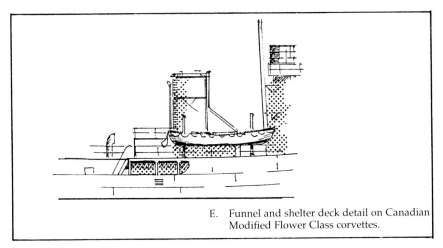

E. Funnel and shelter deck detail on Canadian Modified Flower Class corvettes.

Liferafts and boats

Some of the early British corvettes carried slatted liferafts of merchant service pattern and two 16ft transom-sterned lifeboats on traditional radial davits. The Canadian ships, at least at first, carried the boats abreast the funnel, while in British vessels they were slightly further forward. Subsequently naval Carley floats became standard, and the Modified Flowers carried a single 27ft naval whaler on crescent pattern davits to starboard.

Colour scheme

A very comprehensive discussion of the various camouflage schemes used in corvettes, and tips on painting a model, are to be found in the Lynch book listed in the Sources. Preston and Raven's *Flower Class Corvettes* includes colour examples of the patterns used, while Hodges' *Royal Navy Warship Camouflage 1939–45* explains the rationale behind these schemes. The earliest Canadian corvettes were initially painted a uniform grey, but later exhibited various patterns of white and pastel shades of blue and green; one of the most striking was the so-called Western Approaches Scheme proposed by Peter Scott. In the overcast light of the North Atlantic a white ship was less visible, but when the vessel was in bright sunlight the light blue and green panels broke up the outline so as to make accurate identification of the type of ship more difficult for a U-boat commander (the upright funnel was introduced for the same reason: it made immediate assessment of the course of the corvette much more difficult).

Notes for modelmakers

Because so many corvettes were built, with important differences in appearance between ships, and because the appearance of an individual ship could change substantially over its career, modelling a particular ship can present problems. A brief summary of the overall appearance of corvettes follows. The British short forecastle corvette and the ten Canadian-built corvettes with Flower names had a round stern with the casing enclosing the galley and extending aft to frame 93. In Canadian corvettes the casing stopped at frame 89, the stern was squared off, the Oropesa minesweeping gear (including a winch) was fitted on the quarterdeck, and the platform for the 2pdr was further aft than in the British version. Later the compass house was replaced by an open compass platform and the Canadian 'Swick' radar replaced by a Type 271 lantern. By and large, British corvettes had their forecastles extended aft earlier than their Canadian sisters; in eleven RCN corvettes the forecastle was not shortened at all, and some of these survived until the end of hostilities.

The long-forecastle corvette represented by the 1/72 Matchbox/Revell kit can be completed as the British *Bluebell*, the Canadian *Snowberry* or the USS *Saucy*, but substantial 'kit bashing' would be needed to modify it to represent other Canadian corvettes of the same vintage. Details of the appearance of American corvettes like *Saucy* can be found in photographs in Trevor Lenton's *American Gunboats and Minesweepers*: apart from the American camouflage pattern used, the absence of a gun shield on the 4in is the most obvious difference.

The later 'improved' corvettes and the Modified Flower class had increased sheer and flare, a lengthened upper deck and a three-level bridge. The Modified corvettes had a vertical funnel and lacked the four large stokehold ventilators characteristic of their earlier sisters. The casing reached frame 90, some 22in longer than in the short forecastle version, the stern was squared off, and the 2pdr was in the Canadian position. The mounting for the Hedgehog was placed to starboard with the ready-use lockers to port, and the 4in BL gun was replaced by a Mark XIX QF gun of similar calibre, with a smaller shield than the earlier version. The ten Modifieds built in Britain, including four for the RCN, were more or less identical to those from Canadian yards, but were distinguished by a short mainmast, often by a funnel cap, and by the absence of the short shelter deck abreast the funnel shown in the plan of HMCS *Atholl* and in Sketch

E. We believe they also had the squarish stern of the Canadian ships. The two transom-sterned boats standard in the early corvettes were later replaced by one 27ft whaler. The RCN corvettes carried the boats further aft than did their RN sisters.

The lack of precise details of the appearance of the minesweeping winch is noted above. In minesweepers it was normally surrounded by a frame covered with a fitted tarpaulin so that only the warping heads were visible; while there is no evidence that the same practice was followed in corvettes, representing the winch under cover in this way does offer the modelmaker an acceptable way of 'fudging' this problem.

With the exception of HMCS *Sackville*, the Flower class corvettes which played a crucial part in the convoy battles of fifty years ago are now no more than a memory; all have long since gone to the breaker's yard. Built as a stopgap, they were never awe-inspiring warships, and those aboard earned every nickel of their hard-lying money as they endured the wretched living conditions and the misery inflicted by wind and wave in the North Atlantic. Nonetheless, these sturdy little ships occupy a special place in the history of the Battle of the Atlantic and in the remembrance of those who served in them.

Appendix: Construction list

Original Flower class built in the UK
133 ships including *La Bastiase*, which was sunk by a mine on trials in June 1940, a disaster which wiped out most of the Smith's Dock design team.

Modified Flower class built in the UK
Ten ships, mostly commissioned in 1943, with four immediately transferred to the RCN. The forty-two similar ships built in Canadian yards are considered below. With slightly reduced freeboard amidships, the Modified Flowers had substantially greater draught and displacement than the earlier vessels, and with increased sheer and flare forward were much handsomer. In photographs, they can readily be distinguished from the earlier corvettes, even those in an 'improved' configuration, by the upright mast and funnel and the conspicuous absence of the four tall stokehold ventilators of their predecessors; this gave them a cleaner look than the earlier ships.

Original Flower class built in Canada
Sixty-four ships, including ten built to RN specifications and 'lent' to the RN, which were sailed to the UK in partially finished condition for completion. All had Scotch boilers, and the fifty-four ships remaining under RCN operational control were modified for Oropesa sweeping. A further six short-forecastle ships, similar but lacking minesweeping capability, were built under the 1940–41 programme and commissioned between November 1941 and March 1942.

Ten further 'Revised' corvettes were built under the 1940–41 programme; the first, *Halifax*, was commissioned in November 1941. These Improved ships had long forecastles from the outset, and their hulls, with more sheer and flare and greater rake to the stem, were 3ft longer than those of the earlier ships. All sixteen ships from this programme had watertube boilers, but retained the tall stokehold ventilators. The commanding officer's cabin was moved onto the upper deck, giving a three-level bridge which is very conspicuous in photographs. Pictures of *Lotus*, *Vetch*, *Honeysuckle*, and *Thyme* confirm that this bridge configuration was occasionally also found in RN corvettes.

Canadian Revised corvette 'IE' 1942–43 and 1943–44 programmes
The forty-two ships of this group were essentially identical to the RN Modified class. The initials IE stand for Increased Endurance. Twenty-seven served in the RCN and a further fifteen were built under Reverse Lend-Lease for America, of which in the event only eight went to the USA and the remaining seven to the RN. Four British-built Modifieds were transferred to the RCN.

Castle class
Forty-four ships, all built in the UK. Although these vessels were described as corvettes, and indeed used the same engines as the Flowers, they are outside the scope of this book since they represented a new design. Nearly forty of this type were ordered in Canada, but in the end all were cancelled. The twelve Castles which served in the RCN were all built in Britain.

Although the bulk of these corvettes did duty in the RN and the RCN, eighteen served in the USN, and others served in the naval forces of Norway, France, the Netherlands, Greece, India, New Zealand and Yugoslavia. Even the Kriegsmarine had its Flowers: four partly-built hulls, still on the stocks when France was overrun, were completed as the *U-jäger* (subchasers) PA 1–4. Photographs of these in the possession of Dr Dieter Jung confirm that as completed they were more generously equipped with flak than their Allied sisters, but were still easily recognisable as Flowers. They will be described in the forthcoming Volume 8 of *Die deutschen Kriegsschiffe 1815–1945*, the revision of Erich Gröner's classic work by Dr Jung and Martin Maass. All in all, a total of 270 corvettes were built (145 in England, 121 in Canada and 4 in France), making them the largest class of warships ever built, and they served in more wartime navies than any other type before or since.

HMCS *Agassiz*'s insignia — a grizzly bear holding a U-boat — worn on her 4in gun shield.

THE PHOTOGRAPHS

An atmospheric shot of *Battleford*, close sister to *Agassiz*. *Ken R Macpherson Collection*

Agassiz early in her career. Note the overall grey colour and the lack of armament on the platform, aft. *Ken R Macpherson Collection*

A broadside view of *Agassiz*, probably taken at the same time as the preceding picture, while she was on trials. *National Archives of Canada*

New Westminster was built under the 1940–41 Building Programme and commissioned a year after *Agassiz*. Her foremast is stepped forward of the bridge and there is no mainmast. The absence of large minesweeping davits aft indicates that she was not fitted for sweeping. *Ken R Macpherson Collection*

Also built during the 1940–41 Programme, *Vancouver* was commissioned in March 1942. This is a nice clear shot, showing her as almost identical to *Agassiz*. *Ken R Macpherson Collection*

Agassiz after her refit in early 1943. Note the struts supporting the extensions of the wings of the bridge and that the forecastle has not been extended. The compass house has been retained and a radar lantern added. The mainmast has been removed and the foremast shifted abaft the bridge. A searchlight platform has been added just forward of the 2pdr platform. Further minor alterations include relocation of the galley funnel and the addition of extra Carley floats, reflecting an increase in the size of the crew. She retains her 16ft dinghies. *Ken R Macpherson Collection*

These two snapshots were also taken just after *Agassiz*'s 1943 refit, and while they are not particularly informative, they are of interest as they are from the personal collection of Captain (Lt) B D L Johnson, *Agassiz*'s first Commanding Officer. *Captain B D L Johnson Collection, courtesy of the Vancouver Maritime Museum*

A stern view of an unidentified corvette taken in Toronto in 1941. This ship is probably *Oakville*, but in any event she is a close sister to *Agassiz*. The minesweeping fairleads and depth charge chutes show very clearly at the stern, as do the sweeping davits and part of the winch. *Ken R Macpherson Collection*

Were it not for the pennant number this ship, *Battleford*, could readily be *Agassiz*. Note that a pair of light calibre machine guns have been substituted for the 2pdr in the bandstand aft. *Ken R Macpherson Collection*

An aerial view of *Chicoutimi* taken in October, 1943. *Agassiz* would have looked exactly like this after her first big refit. *Ken R Macpherson Collection*

The stern of a corvette under construction. The bolts that hold the plates in place prior to riveting show very clearly and the chalk designations on the plates, PF1 and APF2 ('F' for the strake and '1' and '2' for the plates) correspond with those shown on the shell expansion in the drawings. *Marine Museum of the Great Lakes at Kingston*

A 2750hp Marine engine ready for installation on the corvette *Drumheller*. The photo was taken on 2 July 1941 and the engine's size is nicely demonstrated by the man on the left. *Marine Museum of the Great Lakes at Kingston*

The stern of an unidentified corvette undergoing a refit. The photo was taken on 30 June 1941. *Marine Museum of the Great Lakes at Kingston*

Details of the after side of *Sackville*'s anchor winch. *John Harland Collection*

A depth charge being loaded into a thrower aboard *Agassiz*. (The name board is just visible to the right of the charge.) *National Archives of Canada*

Another shot of the 4in gun that also shows the fittings of the forecastle deck. Note that the deck has been newly planked over the seamen's mess. *Marine Museum of the Great Lakes at Kingston*

A 4in Breech Loading Mark IX gun. A lot of detail can be made out which would not be seen once the shield was installed. Note the hinged stanchions and shell holders on the platform. *Marine Museum of the Great Lakes at Kingston*

Agassiz after her refit of 1944. She now has an extended forecastle, open bridge and a 27ft whaler. *Ken R Macpherson Collection*

Timmins (in the foreground) was built a year later than *Agassiz* but underwent the same sort of changes during refits. Note the open bridge and the steps up on to the galley roof. *Ken R Macpherson Collection*

Sackville's hedgehog mounting. *John Harland Collection*

The firing mechanism of a Mark IV depth charge thrower as currently fitted aboard *Sackville*. *Agassiz*'s original throwers were of a simpler pattern, lacking the recoil cylinders seen here. *John Harland Collection*

This aerial view of *Snowberry*, taken in 1943, shows the way the depth charge racks were arranged with the round stern. Notice that the 2pdr platform is placed further forward than in the Canadian corvettes. *Ken R Macpherson Collection*

Both *Agassiz* and *Vancouver*, shown here, had this configuration after refits. *Ken R Macpherson Collection*

A remarkably clear photograph of *Smilax* (K-280) a Revised Flower class corvette (Increased Endurance). These vessels are easily identified by their lack of stokehold vents. The upper tier of the two-level depth charge rack is clearly seen. *Marine Museum of the Great Lakes at Kingston/Ken R Macpherson Collection*

Riviere du Loup, an Increased Endurance Flower of the 1942–43 Building Programme and a sister to *Athol*, looking rather weather worn. *Ken R Macpherson Collection*

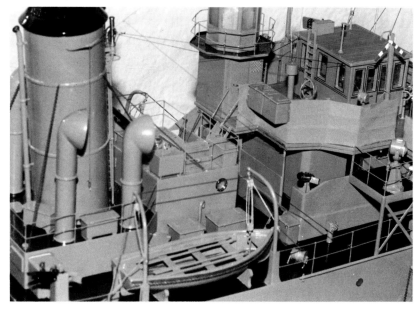

A model of a Norwegian corvette. Note the raised galley between the bridge and funnel. *John Harland Collection, courtesy of the Royal Norwegian Navy Museum, Horten*

A photo of *Forest Hill* taken in 1943. This Improved Endurance corvette was built in Britain as HMS *Ceanothus*, but was transferred to the RCN. The short shelter deck abreast the funnel seen in the Canadian Reviseds is missing in the British-built Revised corvettes. This may be related to the fact that their 16ft dinghies were installed a little further forward than the 27ft whaler in the Canadian version. *Ken R Macpherson Collection*

The Castle class *Kincardine*, built at Middlesbrough in 1944 as HMS *Tamworth Castle*; she was transferred to the RCN in June 1944. *Ken R Macpherson Collection*

THE DRAWINGS

Large scale copies of the drawings reproduced in this book can be obtained from the author. Details from: John McKay, PO Box 752, Fort Langley, British Columbia, Canada V1M 2S2, email: johnwmckay@telus.net.

A General arrangement

A1 GENERAL ARRANGEMENT

A1/1 Outboard profile (1/192 scale)

A1/1

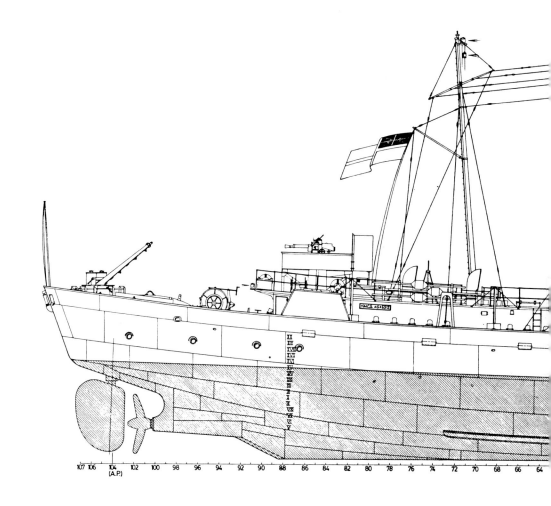

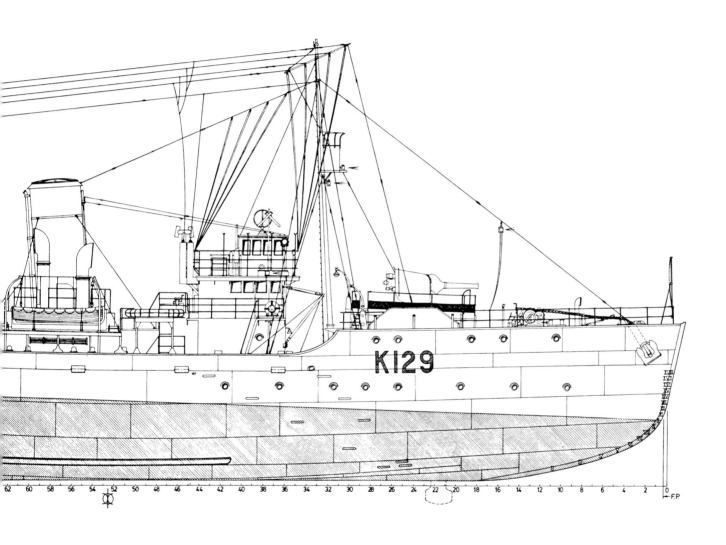

A General arrangement

A1/2   View from forward (1/144 scale)

A1/2

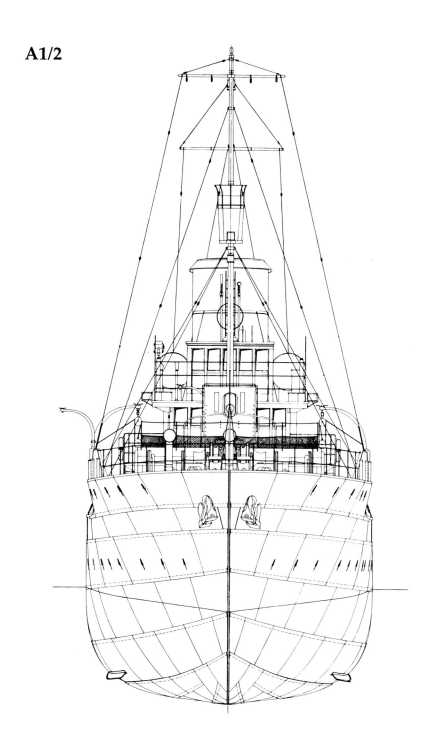

A1/3   View from aft (1/144 scale)

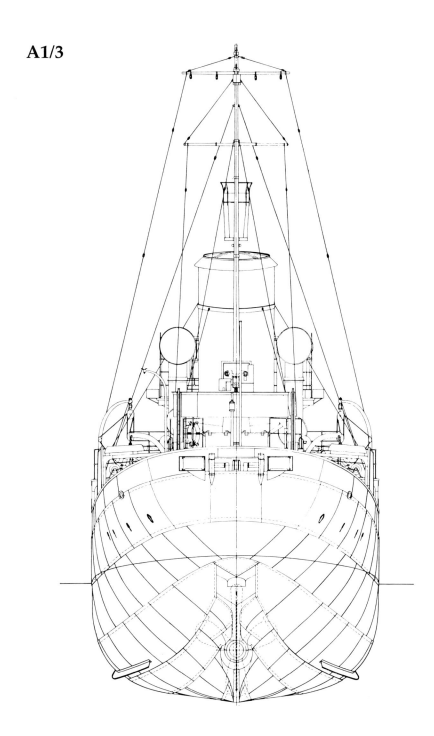

A1/3

A General arrangement

A1/4   Internal profile (1/192 scale)

A1/4

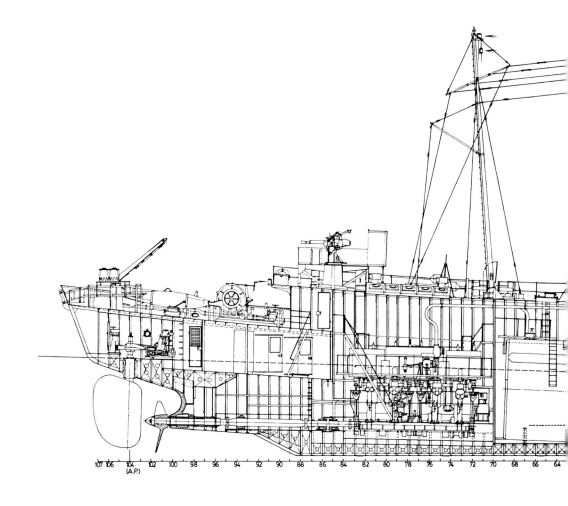

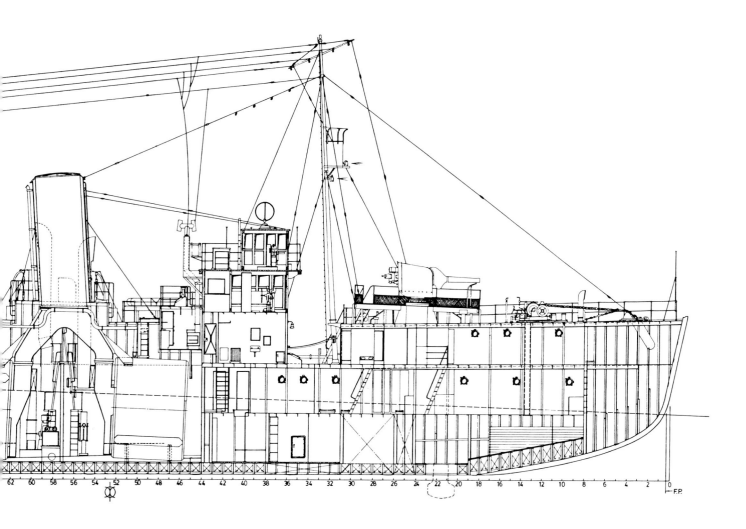

A General arrangement

A2   LINES

A2/1 Sheer plan (1/192 scale)

A2/2 Half breadth plan (1/192 scale)

A2/3 Body plan (1/192 scale)

Length overall	205ft 2¼in
Length between perpendiculars	190ft 0in
Breadth (moulded)	33ft 0in
Breadth (extreme)	33ft 2in
Depth (moulded)	17ft 6in
Depth of hold	16ft 5½in

A2/1

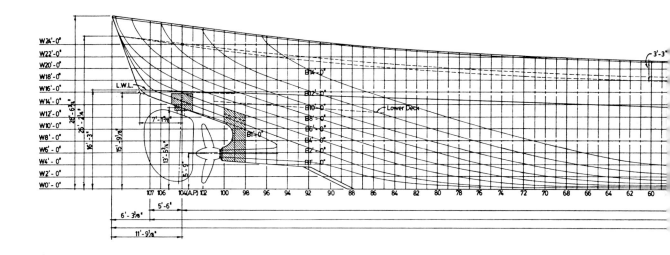

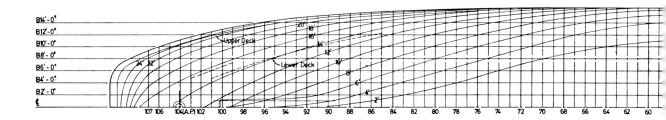

A2/2

A2/3

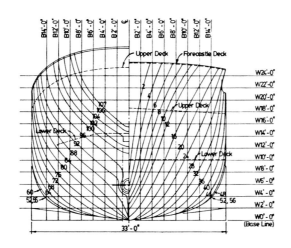
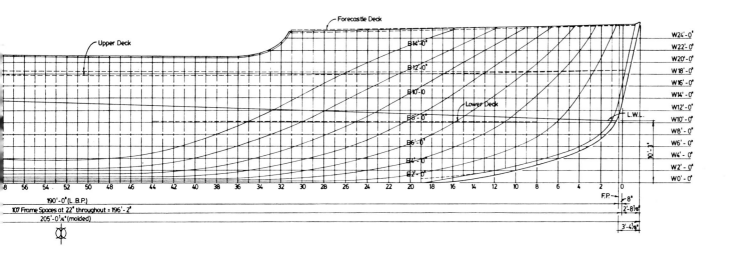
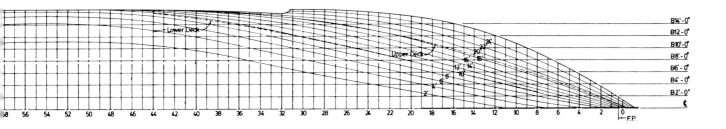

A General arrangement

*A2/4 Plan showing stern variations
(1/96 scale)*

*A2/5 Profile of bow showing increased sheer
(1/192 scale)*

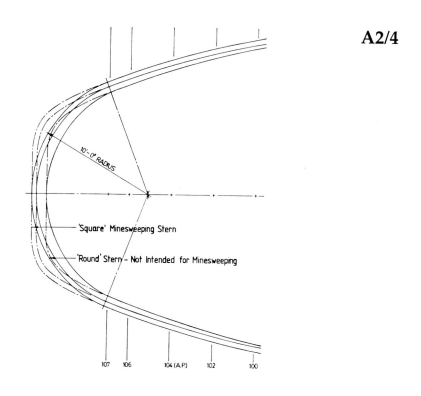

A2/4

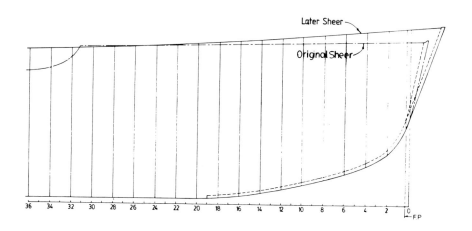

A2/5

A2/6 Plan of bow showing increased flare (1/192 scale)

A2/7 Body plan showing increased sheer and flare (1/96 scale)

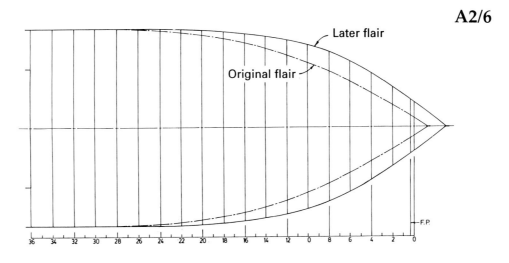

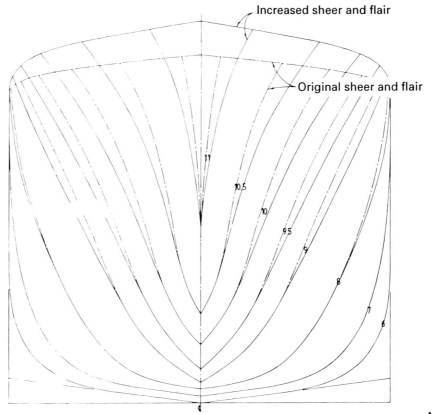

A General arrangement

A2/8 Isometric view of body lines – looking aft (no scale)

A2/9 Isometric view of body lines – looking forward (no scale)

A2/8

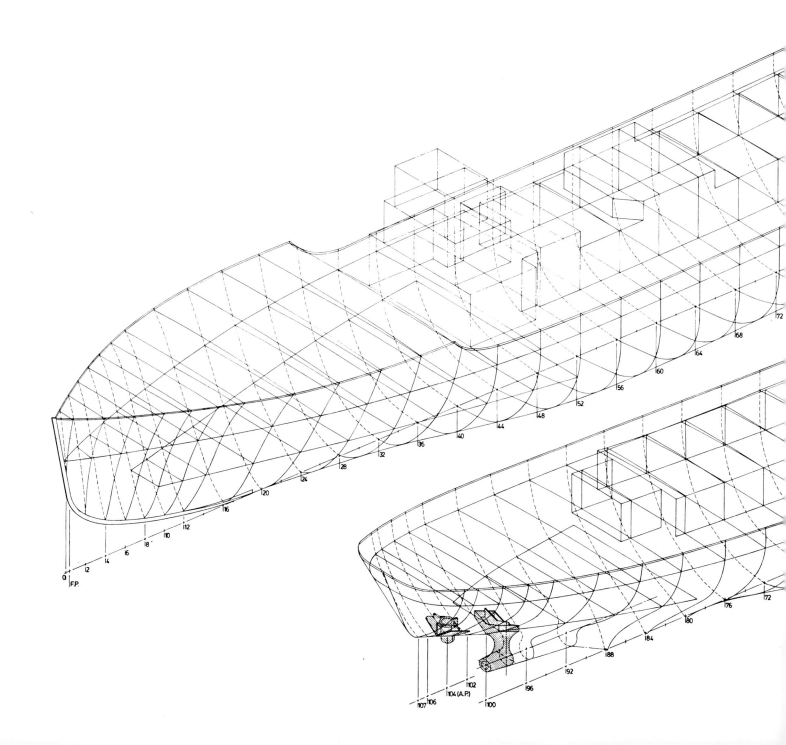

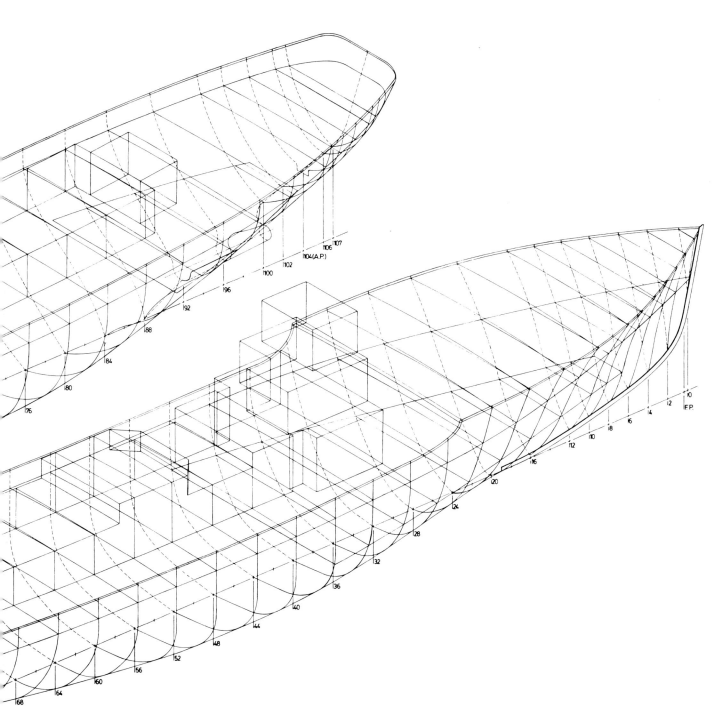

A2/9

A General arrangement

A3   DECK LAYOUTS (1/192 scale)

A3/1   Forecastle and bridge decks

1   Jackstaff (portable)
2   Hawse holes
3   Anchor windlass
4   Cowl vent
5   Bollard
6   Fairlead
7   Splinter protection plate
8   Davit (port and starboard)
9   4in gun
10 Ready-use ammunition locker
11 Kedge anchor (under gun platform)
12 Depression stop
13 Ammunition davit
14 Foremast and bracket
15 Belfry
16 Wheelhouse
17 Chart table
18 Settee (with curtain)
19 Wheel and telemotor
20 Bulletproof shelter
21 Telegraph
22 Compass over
23 W/T office
24 Long wave transmitter
25 Short wave transmitter
26 Sounding boom and carrier
27 Sounding machine
28 Galley skylight
29 Battery box
30 Darkening ship screening locker
31 Galley stack
32 Carley float
33 10cwt derrick boom (port and starboard)
34 Fire buckets
35 Air hatch
36 Davit
37 Life belt rack
38 Funnel casing top
39 Funnel
40 Boiler room vent
41 Stokehold companion
42 Fireworks tank
43 16ft dinghy
44 Fixed davit over DC thrower
45 Mainmast
46 Purchase reels (4)
47 Engine room skylight
48 Engine room vents (4)
49 Dan buoy davit
50 Dan buoys
51 Wash deck locker
52 Aft gun platform
53 2pdr gun
54 Kite/otter
55 Spare otter board
56 Ready-use ammunition locker
57 Reel (under platform)
58 Shelter

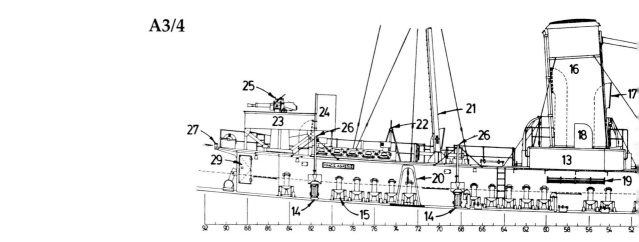

A3/4

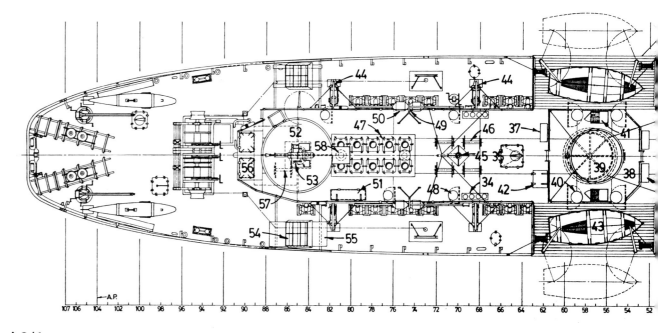

A3/1

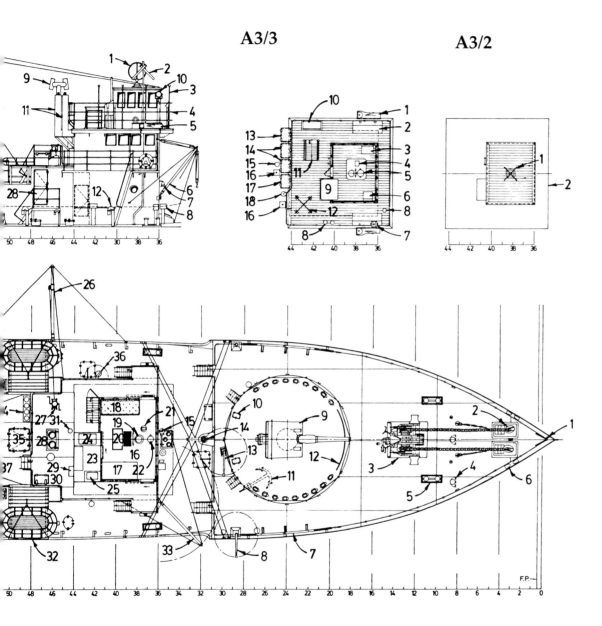

A3/2 Compass house top

1. D/F loop
2. Compass platform below

A3/3 Compass platform

1. Bowlight box
2. Hinged platform
3. Hinged chart table
4. Recorder
5. Asdic wheel lock (compass)
6. Hinged seat
7. 10in signalling lamp (port and starboard)
8. Voice pipe
9. Chart table
10. Flag locker
11. Ladder
12. Conning tower (¾in mild steel)
13. Box for NUC balls
14. Boxes for recognition lights
15. Galley stack
16. Aerial trunk
17. Box for steam signal cones
18. Funnel for answering pendant

A3/4 Engine room casing

1. D/F loop
2. Hand semaphore (port and starboard)
3. Awning stanchion
4. Rail (note canvas dodger mats around compass platform)
5. Bowlight box
6. 10cwt derrick boom
7. Belfry
8. Mushroom vent
9. Galley stack
10. 10in signalling lamp
11. Aerial trunks
12. Fuel tank vent
13. Funnel casing top
14. Depth charge thrower
15. Depth charge stowage
16. Funnel
17. Boiler room vent
18. Stokehold companion
19. Collision mat rack
20. Hinged gallows
21. Mainmast
22. Dan buoy davit
23. Aft gun platform
24. Shelter
25. 2pdr gun
26. Fixed davit over DC thrower
27. Overtaking light
28. Door to galley
29. Door to lobby

A General arrangement

A3/5 Upper deck

1. Paint and lamp room
2. Shelves
3. GI rack
4. Seamen's mess (twenty-six men)
5. Ditty box, hat and boot shelf
6. Seat locker
7. Table
8. Seat
9. Hammock bin
10. Drinking water
11. Mess rack
12. Chain pipe
13. Companion
14. GM lockers
15. Refrigerator
16. Shelf over for refrigerator condenser unit
17. WCs
18. Dirty clothes locker
19. Crew's washplace
20. Shower
21. Companion and skylights
22. Provision issue room
23. Vegetable bin and beef screen
24. Asdic dome stowage
25. Canteen
26. POs' washroom
27. POs' WC
28. Ladder
29. Lock box for magazine flooding valves
30. Foremast
31. Wardroom skylight
32. Hatch
33. Asdic winch
34. 10cwt derrick boom
35. Canvas screen
36. Sounding boom and carrier
37. Bollard
38. Hatch
39. Watertight manhole
40. Officers' WC
41. Lobby
42. Officers' bathroom
43. CO's cabin
44. Berth (drawers under)
45. Galley
46. Sink
47. Galley range
48. Forward boiler room
49. Aft boiler room
50. Engine room
51. Depth charge stowage
52. Depth charge thrower
53. Hinged gallows
54. 5in Downton hand pump
55. Officers' bathroom
56. Lobby
57. Minesweeping winch
58. Winch engine
59. Watertight hatch
60. Minesweeping float
61. Minesweeping davit
62. Otter board
63. Minesweeping fairlead
64. Depth charge rails

A3/5

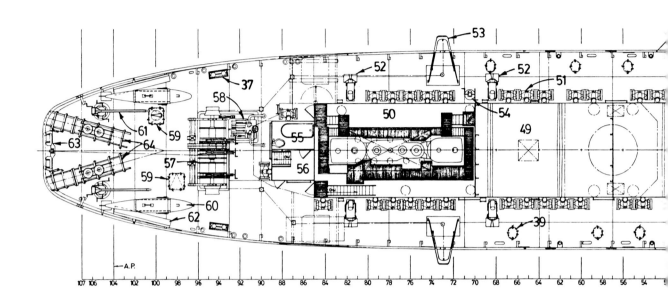

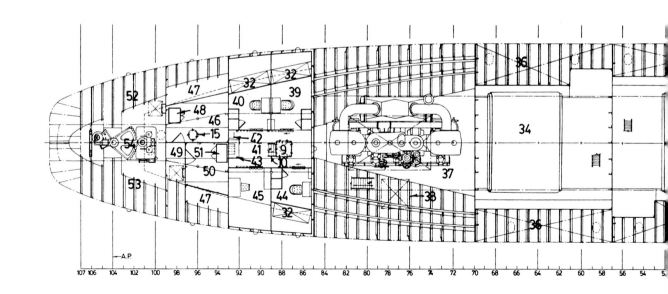

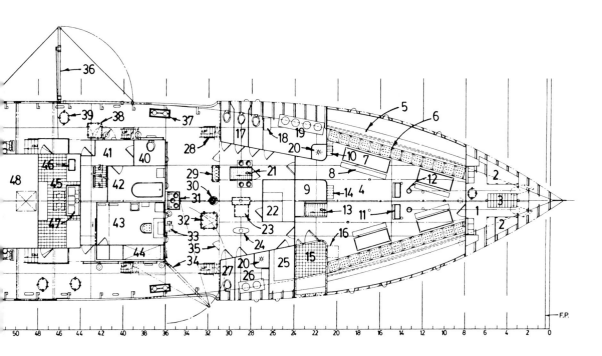
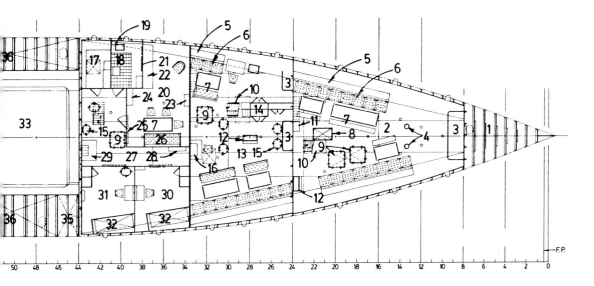

A3/6 Lower deck

1. Fore peak
2. Stokers' mess (sixteen men)
3. Hammock bin
4. Chain pipes
5. Ditty box, hat and boot shelf
6. Seat locker
7. Table and seat
8. Asdic trunk
9. Watertight hatches
10. Ladder
11. Drinking water
12. Mess rack
13. CPOs' and POs' mess (nine men)
14. Cupboards
15. Watertight manhole
16. Desk
17. Officers' store
18. Pantry
19. Sink and 3 gal hot water boiler
20. Wardroom
21. Serving hatch
22. Sideboard
23. Pistol locker
24. Bookcase
25. Notice board
26. Settee
27. Lobby
28. Rifle rack
29. Strong box (GM locker over)
30. Cabin No 1
31. Cabin No 2
32. Berth (drawers under)
33. Forward boiler room
34. Aft boiler room
35. Galley stove oil tank
36. Oil fuel tank
37. Engine room
38. ¾in mild steel bullet proof plate over engine room controls
39. Cabin No 4
40. Cabin No 5
41. Lobby
42. Demolition locker
43. Linen cupboard (GM lockers over)
44. Cabin No 3
45. Office
46. Provision room
47. Shelf
48. Bread locker
49. Lobby
50. No 1 store
51. Loan clothing locker
52. Steering gear flat
53. Minesweeping store
54. Steering engine

A3/6

A General arrangement

A3/7 Hold

1. Fore peak
2. Chain locker
3. Cable clench
4. Store
5. Asdic compartment
6. Fresh water tank
7. Reserve feed water tank
8. Spirit room
9. Lobby
10. 4in magazine
11. Shell room
12. Stringer
13. Oil fuel tank
14. 2pdr magazine
15. Save all
16. Forward boiler room
17. Aft boiler room
18. Engine room
19. Engine base (bed plate)
20. Engineers' ready-use store
21. Engineers' store
22. Shelves
23. After peak
24. Propeller bracket
25. Rudder bearing

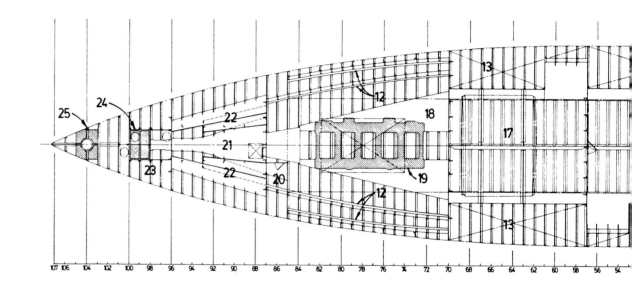

A3/7

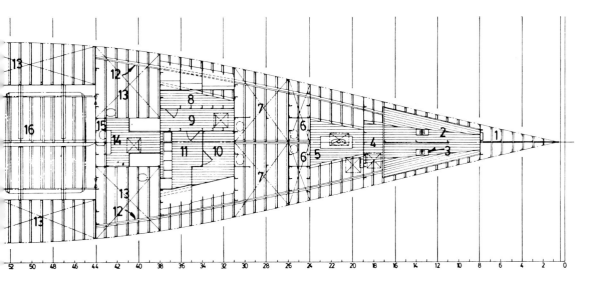

A General arrangement

*A3/8 Plan of bridge as modified, March 1944
(1/192 scale)*

1   Line of forecastle deck
2   20mm Oerlikon
3   Wind deflector
4   A/S hut
5   Recess for chart table
6   Compass
7   Pelorus
8   18in high platform
9   Oerlikon RU locker
10 Steam signal cones
11 NUC signal balls
12 NUC lights
13 RDF office
14 Flag lockers
15 10in signalling lamp
16 6in high platform

*A3/9 Plan of forecastle deck as modified
(1/192 scale)*

1   Fairlead
2   Hawse pipes
3   Anchor windlass
4   4in gun
5   Ammunition davit
6   Companion
7   Ammunition hatch
8   Hedgehog mounting
9   Ribbed platform
10 Wheelhouse
11 Hatch
12 Sounding boom
13 Lifebelt rack
14 Galley funnel
15 Air hatch
16 Vegetable locker
17 Hatch
18 Boiler room vent
19 Sounding machine
20 Carley floats
21 27ft whaler
22 Beef screen
23 Reel
24 DC davit
25 Engine room vent
26 Engine room skylight
27 Searchlight platform
28 2pdr gun
29 Collision mat rack

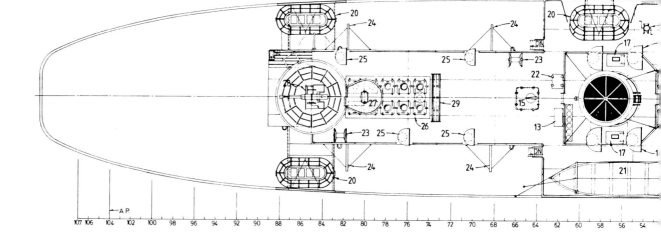

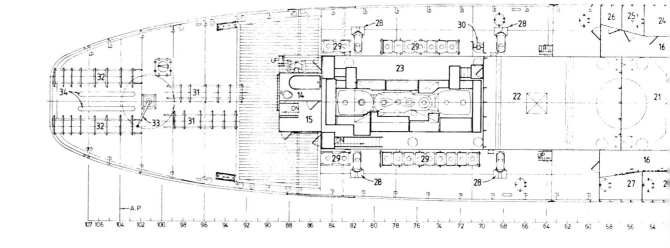

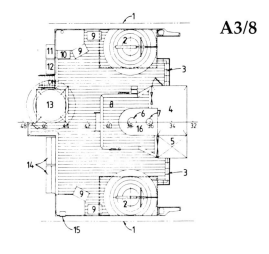

A3/8

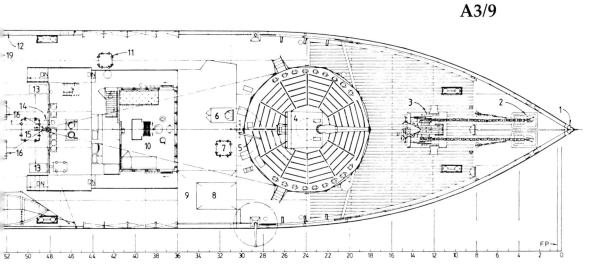

A3/9

A3/10 Plan of upper deck as modified (1/192 scale)

1. Main naval store
2. Seamen's mess
3. Provision room
4. Crew's washplace
5. WC
6. Shower
7. Refrigerator
8. Canteen
9. POs' washplace
10. POs' WC
11. Low power room
12. CO's cabin
13. Officers' bathroom
14. Officers' WC
15. Lobby
16. Passage
17. Dispensary
18. Ship's office
19. Hammocks
20. Galley
21. Forward boiler room
22. Aft boiler room
23. Engine room
24. Issue room
25. Lamp room
26. Paint room
27. Cabin
28. DC thrower
29. Reload DCs
30. 5in Downton pump
31. Reload DC rails
32. DC rails
33. DC davit
34. Hinged platform

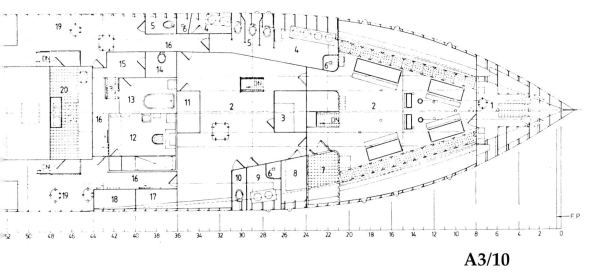

A3/10

A General arrangement

A4   ISOMETRIC VIEWS (no scale)

A4/1 *Isometric view from aft*

A4/1

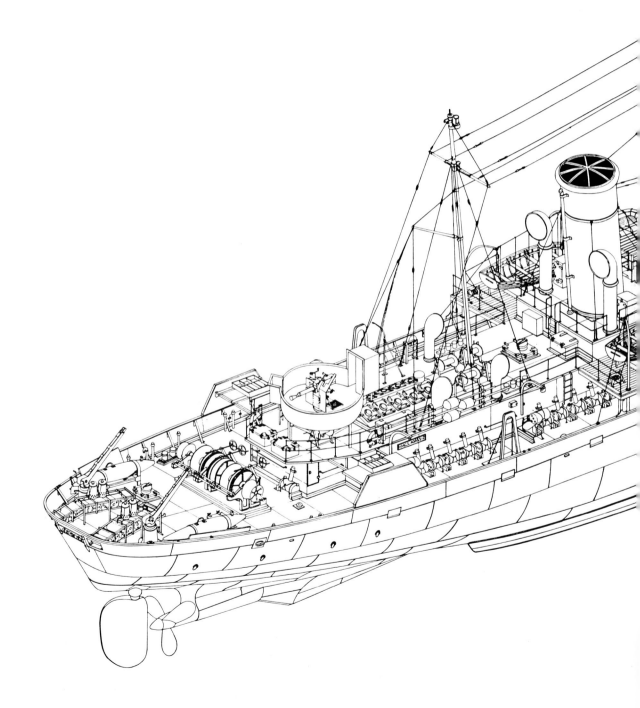

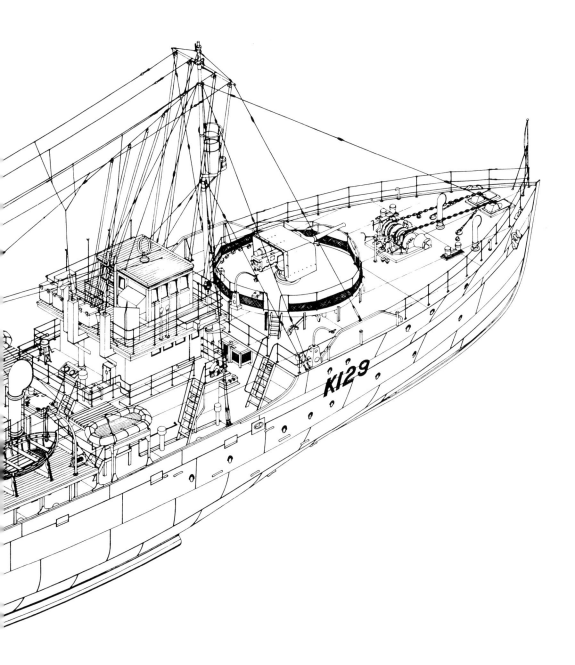

A General arrangement

A4/2 Isometric view from forward

A4/2

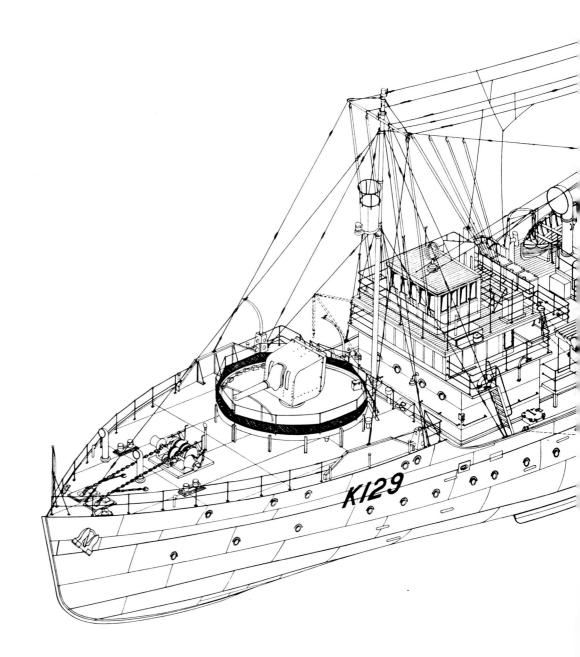

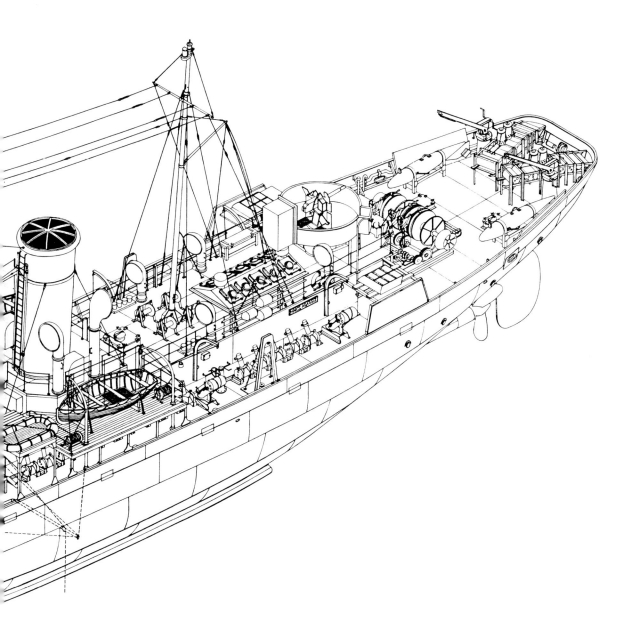

B Internal hull

B1 INTERNAL PROFILE (1/96 scale)

B1/1 Internal profile – aft

1. W/T office
2. Sounding machine
3. Pipe rail (3ft 3in)
4. Galley skylight
5. Carley float
6. Air hatch
7. Ladder
8. Life belt rack
9. Funnel
10. Funnel ladder
11. Boiler room vent
12. Funnel guy
13. Steam release pipe
14. Flexible steel wire rope rail
15. Fire buckets
16. Purchase reel
17. Mainmast
18. Mainmast shroud
19. Mainmast step
20. Main yard braces
21. Dan buoy carrier stanchion
22. Dan buoy davit
23. Dan buoy
24. Engine room vent
25. Mushroom vent
26. Engine room skylight
27. Aft gun platform
28. 2pdr gun
29. Shelter
30. Ready-use ammunition locker
31. Overtaking light
32. Minesweeping winch engine
33. Minesweeping winch
34. Pipe vent
35. Bollard
36. Mooring pipe
37. Minesweeping davit
38. Minesweeping float
39. Watertight hatch
40. Depth charge rails
41. Smoke candles
42. Galley
43. Galley range
44. Cupboard
45. Forward boiler room
46. Aft boiler room
47. Scotch marine boiler
48. Smokebox
49. Smokestack
50. Furnace opening
51. Boiler stool
52. Uptake
53. Steam supply valve
54. 6in steam supply
55. Ladder
56. Grating
57. Watertight bulkhead
58. Main feed pump
59. Sirocco fan
60. Oil fuel pumping and heating unit
61. Engine room
62. Valves
63. 2750hp Marine engine
64. Platform
65. Reversing wheel
66. Throttle wheel
67. Engine bed
68. Thrust shaft
69. Thrust block
70. Shaft tunnel
71. Intermediate shaft
72. Tunnel bearing
73. Tail shaft and stern tube and gland
74. Cast steel propeller bracket
75. Propeller
76. Steel shelves
77. Engineers' store
78. Eye plates (for lifting shaft)
79. After peak
80. Anti-eddying bar
81. Lobby
82. Non-watertight door
83. Lobby
84. Linen cupboards and GM lockers
85. Sliding doors
86. Lobby
87. Loan clothing store
88. Steering gear flat and minesweeping store
89. Steering engine
90. Emergency wheel
91. Rudder bearing
92. Rudder

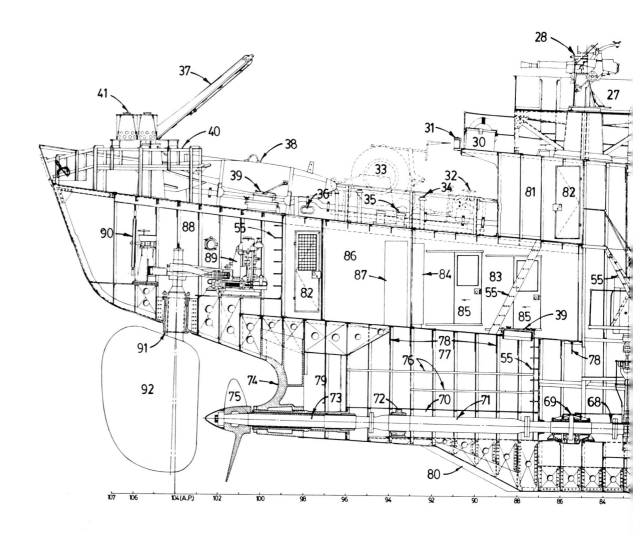

B1/1

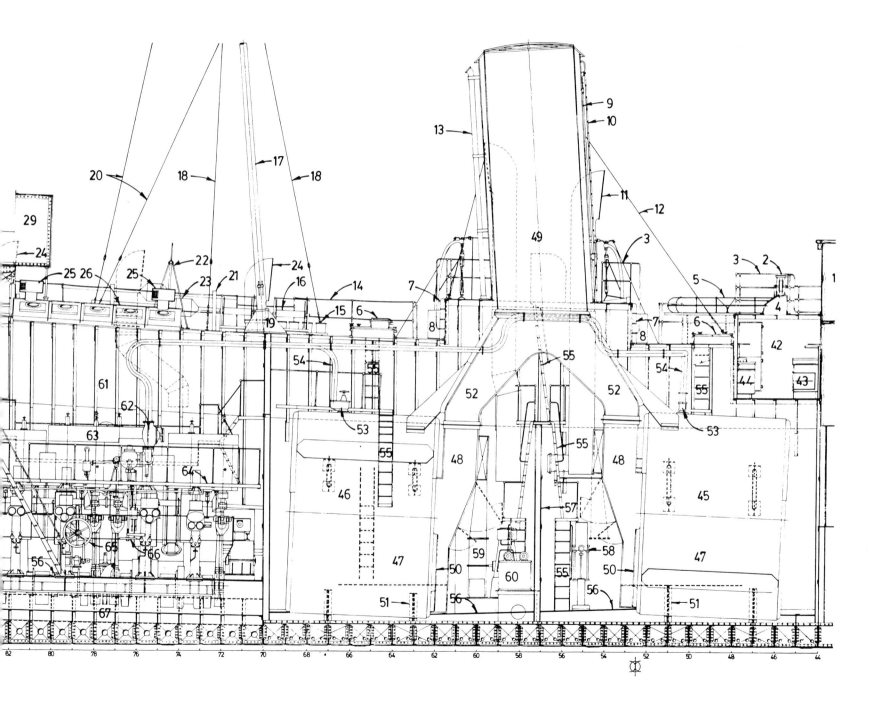

B Internal hull

B1/2 Internal profile – forward

1. Jackstaff (portable)
2. Fore stay
3. Flexible steel wire rope rail
4. Cowl vent
5. Hawse rubber
6. Bottle screw
7. Fairlead
8. Bollard
9. Anchor cable
10. Anchor windlass
11. Voice pipe
12. 4in gun platform
13. Gun mount
14. 4in gun
15. Depression stop
16. Mushroom vent
17. Foremast
18. Foremast shrouds
19. Foremast bracket
20. Foremast step
21. D/F loop
22. Awning stanchion
23. Pipe rail (4ft-3in)
24. Belfry
25. Ladder
26. Galley stack
27. Boxes (4) on compass platform
28. Aerial trunks (2)
29. Flag locker
30. Compass house
31. Asdic wheel lock (compass)
32. Recorder
33. Raised platform
34. Wheel house
35. Bullet proof shelter
36. Bridge telemotor
37. Grating
38. W/T office
39. Long wave transmitter
40. Pipe rail (3ft, 3in)
41. Sounding machine
42. Galley skylight
43. Paint and lamp room
44. Hawse pipe
45. GI rack
46. Watertight manhole
47. Seamen's mess
48. Scuttle
49. Pillar
50. Girder
51. Knee (at side)
52. Seat locker
53. Table
54. Chain pipe
55. Ditty box, hat and boot shelf
56. Mess rack
57. GM locker
58. Hammock bin
59. Provision issue room (with shelves)
60. Companion
61. Skylight
62. Lock box for magazine flooding valves
63. Wardroom skylight
64. Ladder
65. Handrail
66. Officers' bathroom
67. Non-watertight door
68. Lobby
69. Galley
70. Galley range
71. Cupboard
72. Forepeak
73. Asdic trunk
74. Cupboards
75. CPOs' and POs' mess
76. Watertight hatch
77. Plywood bulkhead
78. Wardroom
79. Pistol locker
80. Bookcase
81. Sideboard
82. Noticeboard
83. Lobby
84. Forward boiler room
85. Chain locker
86. Wood flat and lining
87. Cable clench
88. Store
89. Asdic compartment
90. Box for depth charge primer
91. Lockers
92. Demolition charge stowage box on shelf
93. Depth charge on shelf
94. Asdic winch
95. Folding work bench
96. Tool boxes (10in × 15in × 7.5in deep)
97. Fresh water tank
98. Reserve feed water tank
99. Wash plate
100. Stringer
101. 4in magazine
102. Magazine flooding pipes
103. Wood flat
104. Shell room
105. Shelves
106. Watertight door
107. 2pdr magazine
108. Shelf
109. Save all
110. Stem bar
111. Scarph

B1/2

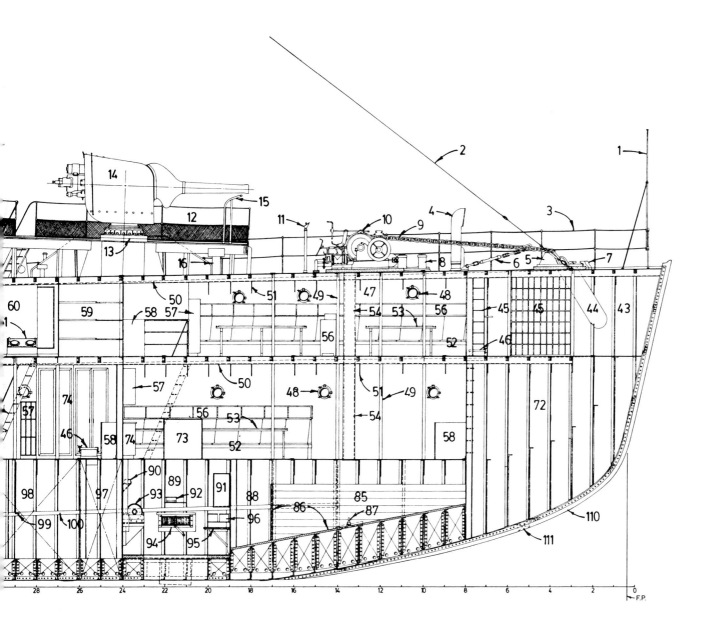

B Internal hull

B1/3 Profile of HMCS Agassiz *as modified*, March 1944 (1/192 scale)

1. Fairlead
2. Main naval store
3. Fore peak
4. Anchor windlass
5. Seamen's mess
6. Stokers' mess
7. Chain locker
8. Store
9. Asdic trunk
10. Watertight hatch
11. Ladder
12. 4in gun
13. A/S davit
14. Ammunition davit
15. D/F coil
16. Splinter protection plate
17. Seamen's mess and washplace
18. Low power room (centre)
19. Asdic compartment
20. Fresh water tank
21. Reserve feed water tanks
22. Magazine and spirit room
23. Magazine and oil fuel tanks
24. Save all
25. Shield at Hedgehog
26. A/S hut
27. 20mm Oerlikon
28. Anchor light
29. Lantern
30. Galley
31. Forward boiler room
32. Aft boiler room
33. Engine room
34. 27ft whaler
35. Galley range funnel
36. Boiler room vents
37. Engine room vents
38. Searchlight platform
39. 2pdr gun
40. Engineers' store
41. Provision room and No 1 store
42. After peak
43. Steering gear compartment
44. Reload DC rails
45. DC davit
46. DC rails

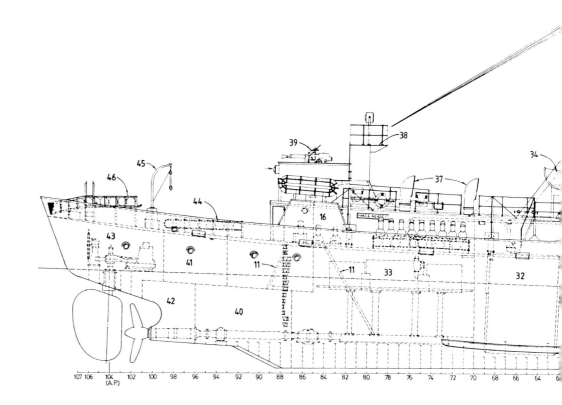

B1/3

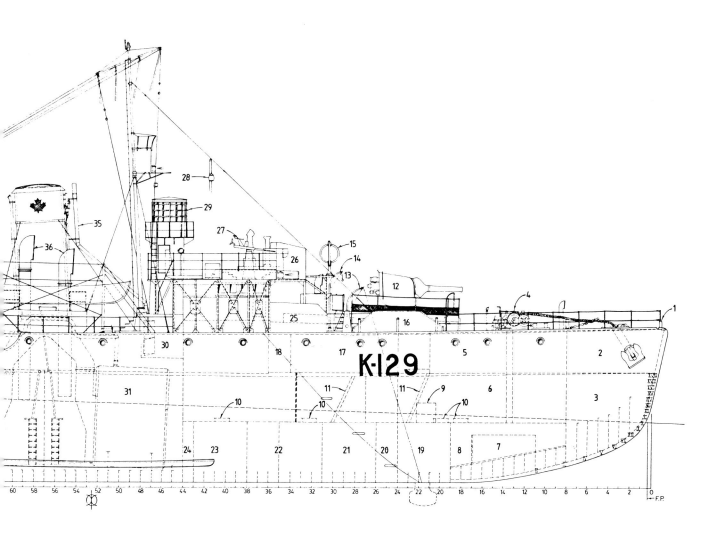

B Internal hull

B2 ISOMETRIC VIEWS (no scale)

B2/1 Isometric view of compass house

B2/2 Isometric view of wheel house

B2/3 Isometric view of forecastle and casing

B2/4 Isometric view of shell

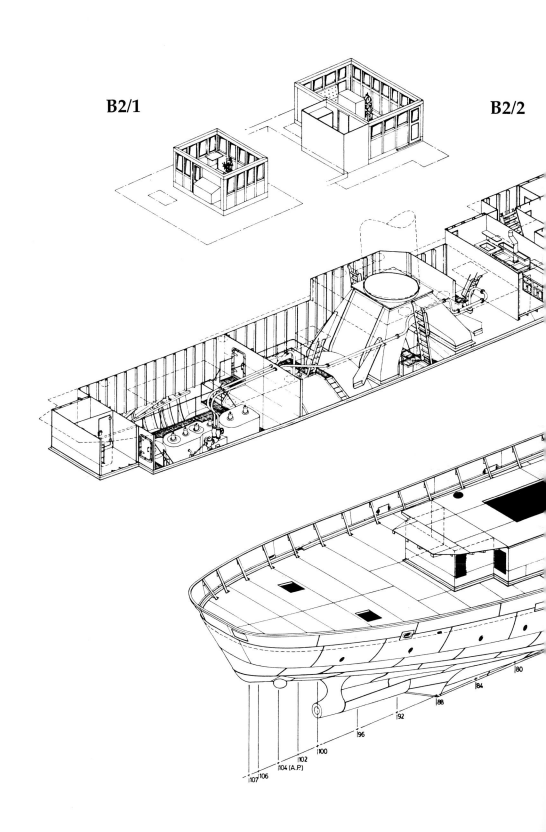

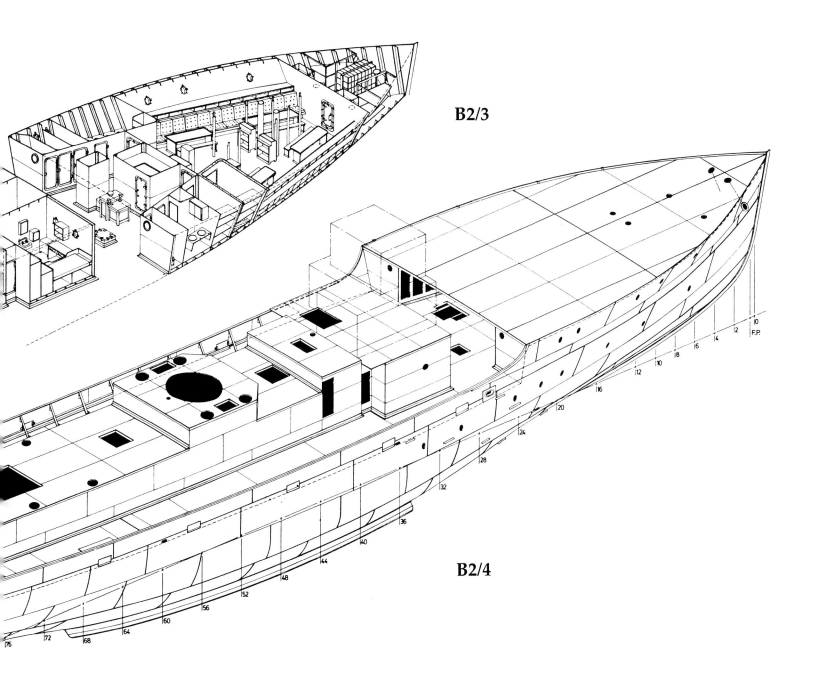

B2/3

B2/4

B Internal hull

B2/5 Isometric view of lower deck

B2/6 Isometric view of hold

B2/5

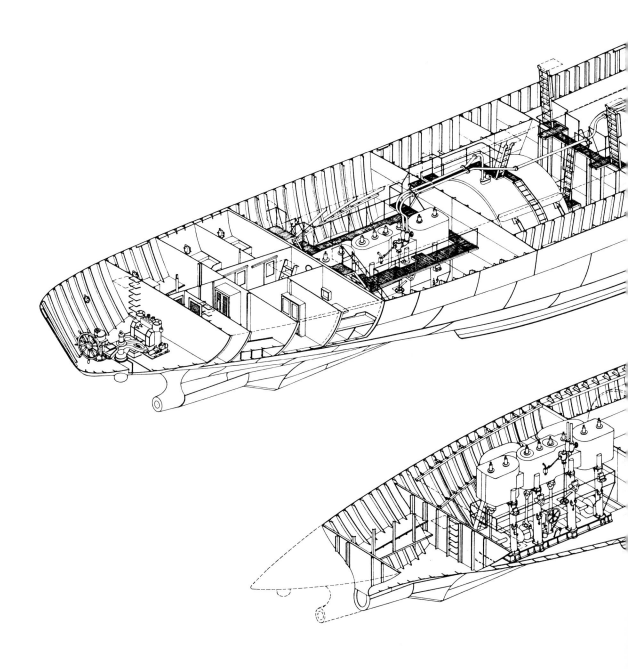

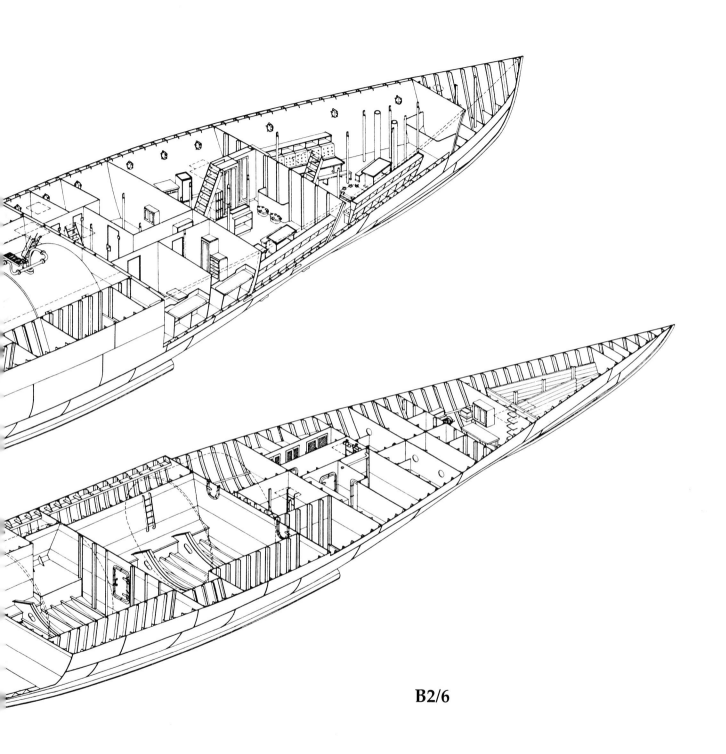

B2/6

B Internal hull

B3 HULL CROSS SECTIONS
(1/96 scale)

B3/1 *Cross section at '4' – looking forward*

1   Jackstaff (portable)
2   Rail
3   Hawse rubber
4   Fairlead
5   Paint and lamp room
6   Shelf
7   Hawse pipe
8   GI racks
9   Fore peak
10 Stem bar

B3/2 *Cross section at '8' – looking aft*

1   Rail
2   Cowl vent
3   Pipe vent
4   Bollard
5   Deck ring
6   Paint and lamp room
7   GI rack
8   Watertight door
9   Watertight manhole
10 Fore peak
11 Ladder

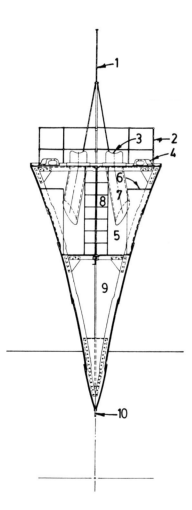

B3/1

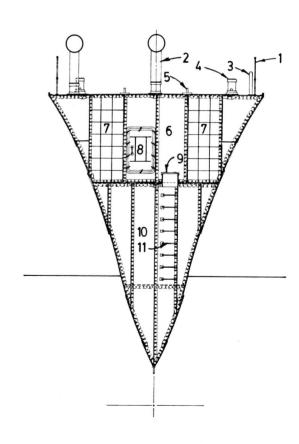

B3/2

B3/3　Cross section at '12' – looking aft

1　Rail
2　Anchor windlass
3　Knee
4　Girder
5　Chain pipe
6　Ditty box, hat and boot shelf
7　Seat locker
8　Table
9　Seat
10　Seamen's mess
11　Stokers' mess
12　Chain locker
13　Wood lining
14　Pillar

B3/4　Cross section at '16' – looking aft

1　Rail
2　Mushroom vent
3　Seamen's mess
4　Knee
5　Girder
6　Pillar
7　Ditty box, hat and boot shelf
8　Table
9　Seat locker
10　Seat
11　Stokers' mess
12　Watertight hatch
13　Chain locker
14　Wood lining

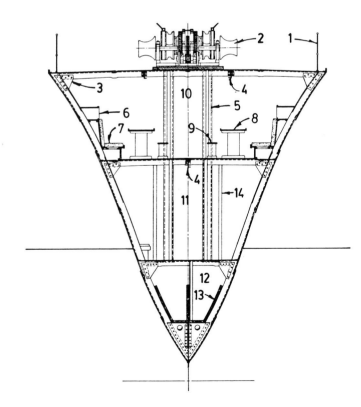

B3/3

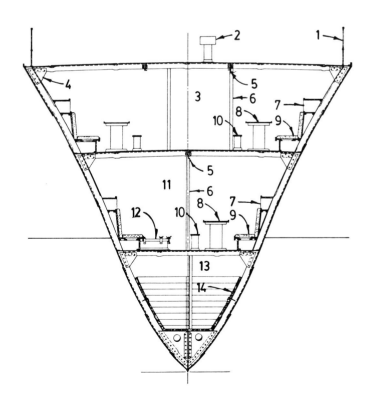

B3/4

B Internal hull

B3/5 Cross section at '20' – looking aft

1. 4in gun
2. Depression stop
3. 4in gun platform
4. Pipe vent
5. Splinter protection plate
6. Seamen's mess
7. Knee
8. Girder
9. Shelf for refrigerator condenser unit
10. GM lockers
11. Ditty box, hat and boot shelf
12. Seat locker
13. Hammock bin
14. Drinking water
15. Stokers' mess
16. Pillar
17. Ladder
18. Asdic trunk
19. Drinking water
20. Table
21. Seat
22. Watertight hatch
23. Asdic compartment
24. Stringer
25. Wooden instrument board
26. Perforated cable tray
27. Box for depth charge primer
28. Depth charge on shelf
29. Heater
30. Asdic winch
31. Wood flat
32. Asdic

B3/6 Cross section at '24' – looking forward

1. 4in gun
2. Depression stop
3. 4in gun platform
4. 4in shell holder
5. Pipe vent
6. Splinter protection plate
7. Mushroom vent
8. Crew's washplace
9. Basin
10. Shower
11. Watertight door
12. Provision issue room
13. Shelves
14. Canteen
15. CPOs' and POs' mess
16. Cupboards
17. Hammock bin
18. Ditty box, hat and boot shelf
19. Seat locker
20. Fresh water tank
21. Wash board
22. Stringer

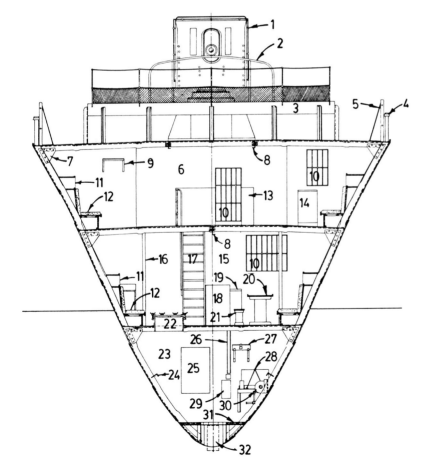

B3/5

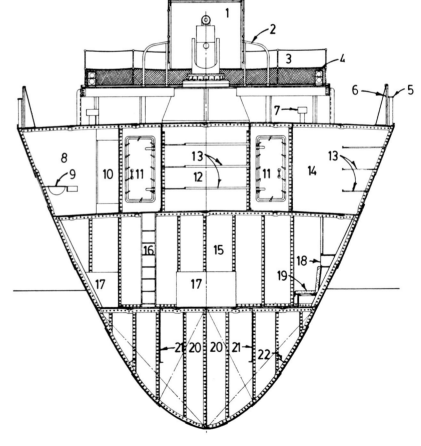

B3/6

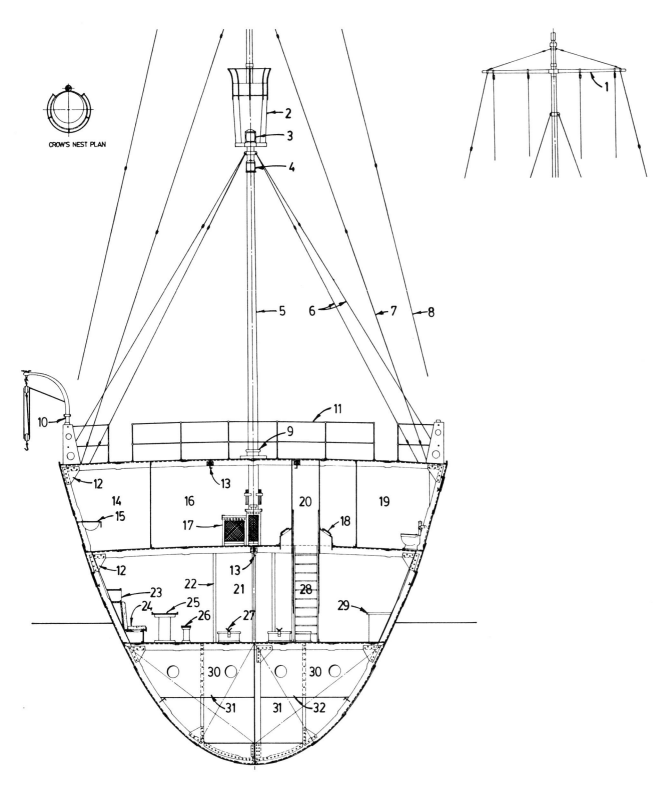

B3/7 Cross section at '28' – looking aft

1. Fore yard
2. Crow's nest
3. Steaming light (electric)
4. Steaming light (oil)
5. Foremast
6. Foremast shrouds
7. Foremast backstays
8. Fore yard braces
9. Foremast bracket
10. Davit
11. Forecastle rail
12. Knee
13. Girder
14. POs' washroom
15. Basin
16. Upper deck
17. Vegetable bin and beef screen
18. Skylight
19. WC
20. Companion
21. CPOs' and POs' mess
22. Pillar
23. Ditty box, hat and boot shelf
24. Seat locker
25. Table
26. Seat
27. Watertight manhole
28. Desk
30. Reserve feed water tank
31. Wash plate
32. Stringer

B3/7

B Internal hull

B3/8 Cross section at '32' – looking forward

1. Fore yard
2. Crow's nest
3. Foremast
4. Jacob's ladder
5. Foremast shrouds
6. Foremast backstay
7. Fore yard brace
8. 4in gun
9. Ammunition davit
10. Davit
11. Forecastle rail
12. Foremast bracket
13. Upper deck
14. Ladder
15. Scuttle
16. Companion
17. Lock box for magazine flooding valves
18. Skylight
19. Vegetable bin and beef screen
20. Watertight hatch
21. Knee
22. Girder
23. CPOs' and POs' mess
24. Pillar
25. Ditty box, hat and boot shelf
26. Seat locker
27. Table
28. Seat
29. Watertight hatch
30. Watertight manhole
31. Spirit cupboard
32. Spirit room
33. Lobby
34. Magazine flooding valves
35. 4in magazine
36. Shelf
37. Wood flat

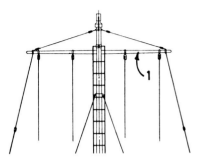
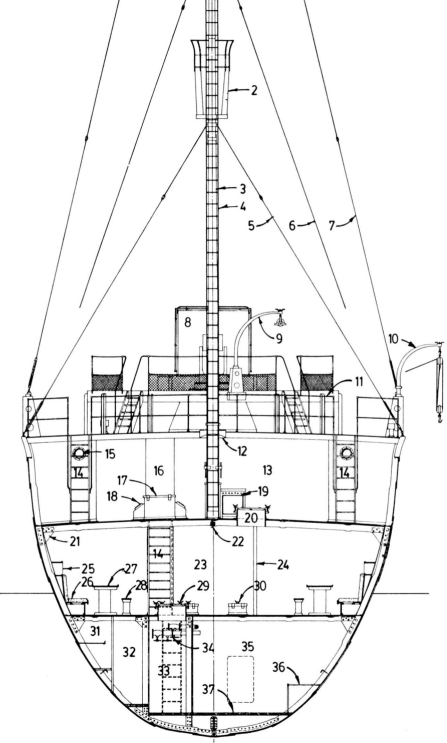

B3/8

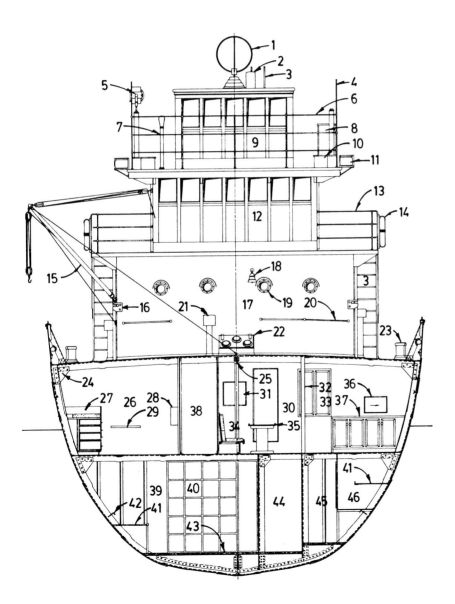

B3/9 Cross section at '36' – looking aft

1. D/F loop
2. Galley stack
3. Ladder
4. Awning stanchion
5. 10in signalling lamp
6. Pipe rail (4ft 3in)
7. Voice pipe
8. Flag locker
9. Compass house
10. Hinged platform
11. Bowlight
12. Wheel house
13. Pipe rail (3ft 3in)
14. Lifebuoy
15. 10cwt derrick boom
16. Derrick boom bracket
17. Upper deck
18. Belfry
19. Scuttle
20. Handrail
21. Mushroom vent
22. Wardroom skylight
23. Bollard
24. Knee
25. Girder
26. Cabin No 1
27. Berth (with drawers)
28. Folding lavatory
29. Folding desk
30. Ward room
31. Notice board
32. Pillar
33. Bookcase
34. Settee
35. Table
36. Serving hatch
37. Sideboard
38. Lobby
39. Shell room
40. Shelves
41. Shelf
42. Stringer
43. Wood flat
44. Lobby
45. Spirit room
46. Rum cupboard

B3/9

B Internal hull

B3/10 Cross section at '40' – looking aft

1. D/F loop
2. Galley stack
3. Ladder
4. Compass house
5. Chart table
6. Awning stanchion
7. Flag locker
8. Voice pipe
9. Wheel house
10. Settee
11. Pipe rail (4ft 3in)
12. Pipe rail (3ft 3in)
13. Curtain
14. Sliding door
15. Carley float
16. Davit
17. Upper deck
18. Mushroom vent
19. Pipe vent
20. Watertight manhole
21. CO's cabin
22. Shelf
23. Berth (drawers under)
24. Radiator
25. Officers' bathroom
26. Lobby
27. Cabin No 2
28. Folding lavatory
29. Drawers
30. Wardrobe
31. Lobby
32. Girder
33. Strong box
34. GM lockers
35. Ladder
36. Pillar
37. Oiltight manhole
38. Pantry
39. 3 gal hot water boiler
40. Sink
41. Hinged seat
42. Watertight hatch
43. Ladder
44. Oil fuel tank
45. Wash plate
46. Stringer
47. 2pdr magazine
48. Shelf
49. Knee

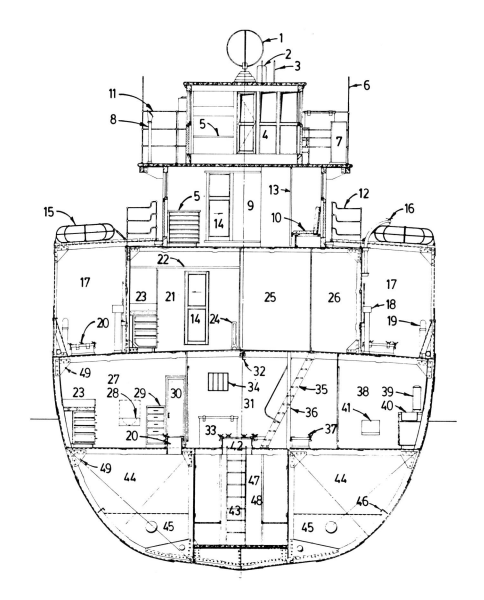

B3/10

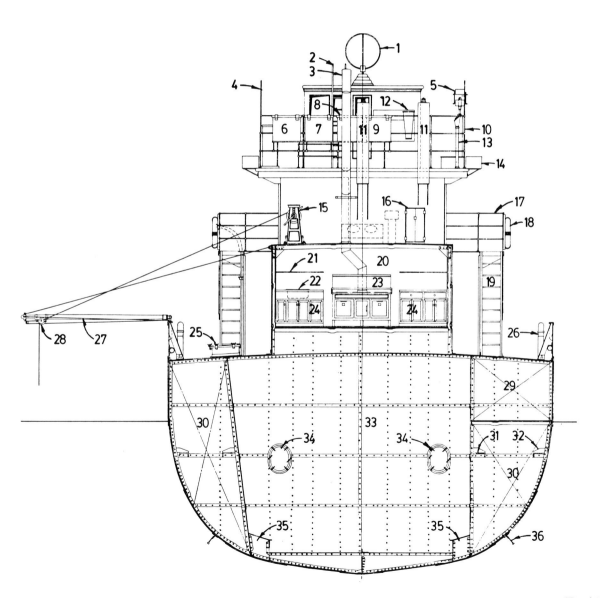

B3/11 Cross section at '44' – looking forward

1. D/F loop
2. Ladder
3. Galley stack
4. Awning stanchion
5. 10in signalling lamp
6. Box for NUC balls
7. Box for recognition lights
8. Box for recognition lights
9. Box for steam signal cones
10. Pipe rail (4ft 3in)
11. Aerial trunk
12. Funnel for answering pendant
13. Voice pipe
14. Bowlight box
15. Sounding machine
16. Battery box
17. Pipe rail (3ft 3in)
18. Lifebuoy
19. Ladder
20. Galley
21. Shelf
22. Sink
23. Galley range
24. Cupboards
25. Watertight manhole
26. Pipe vent
27. Sounding boom
28. Carrier and block
29. Galley stove oil tank
30. Fuel oil tank
31. Bulkhead stringer
32. Stringer
33. Forward boiler room
34. Oiltight manhole
35. Oiltight gutterway
36. Bilge keel

B3/11

B   Internal hull

B3/12 Cross section at '48' – looking aft

1. Carley float
2. Ladder
3. Air hatch
4. Upper deck
5. Pipe rail
6. Galley landing
7. Pipe vent
8. Oil fuel tank
9. Wash plate
10. Knees
11. Stringer
12. Bulkhead stringer
13. Forward boiler room
14. Scotch marine boiler
15. Uptake
16. Steam supply valve
17. Boiler stay
18. Boiler stool
19. Oiltight gutterway
20. Ladder
21. Grating
22. Bilge keel

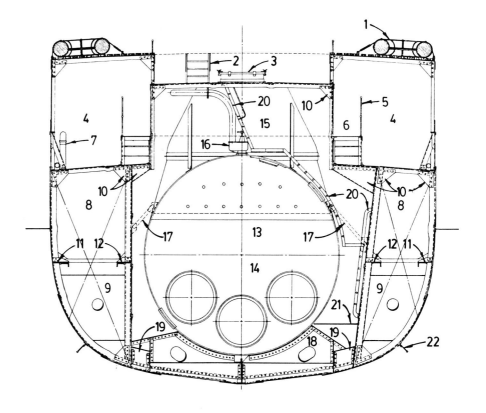

B3/12

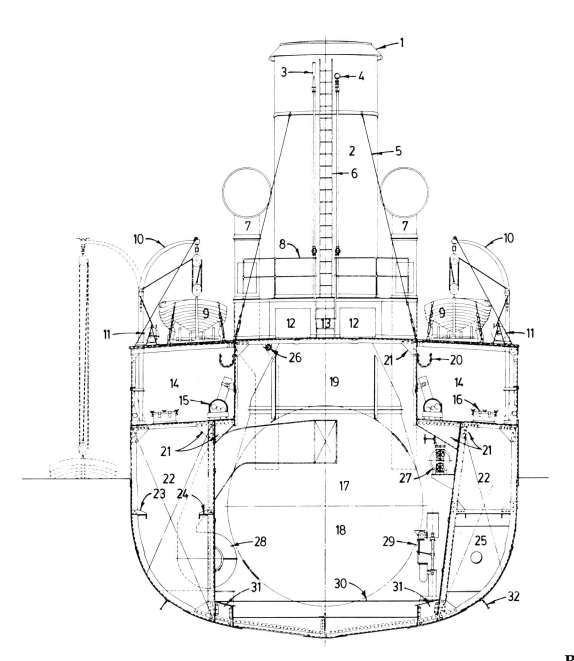

B3/13 *Cross section at '52' – looking aft*

1. Funnel cap
2. Funnel
3. Whistle
4. Siren
5. Funnel guy
6. Funnel ladder
7. Boiler room vent
8. Pipe rail
9. 16ft dinghy
10. Davit
11. Rope reel
12. Life belt rack
13. Ladder
14. Upper deck
15. Depth charge stowage
16. Watertight manhole
17. Forward boiler room
18. Scotch marine boiler
19. Uptake
20. Collision mat rack
21. Knees
22. Oil fuel tank
23. Stringer
24. Bulkhead stringer
25. Wash plate
26. 6in steam supply
27. Exhaust steam feed water heater
28. Sirocco fan
29. Main feed pump
30. Grating
31. Oiltight gutterway
32. Bilge keel

B3/13

B Internal hull

B3/14 *Cross section at '56' – looking aft*

1. Funnel cap
2. Funnel
3. Smokestack
4. Boiler room vents
5. Stokehold companion
6. 16ft dinghy
7. Upper deck
8. Collision mat rack
9. Pipe vent
10. Oiltight manhole
11. Oil fuel tank
12. Bulkhead stringer
13. Stringer
14. Knees
15. Forward boiler room
16. 6in steam supply
17. Uptake
18. Platform
19. Ladder
20. Exhaust steam feed water heater
21. Oil fuel pumping and heating unit
22. Watertight door
23. Grating
24. Oiltight gutterway
25. Bilge keel

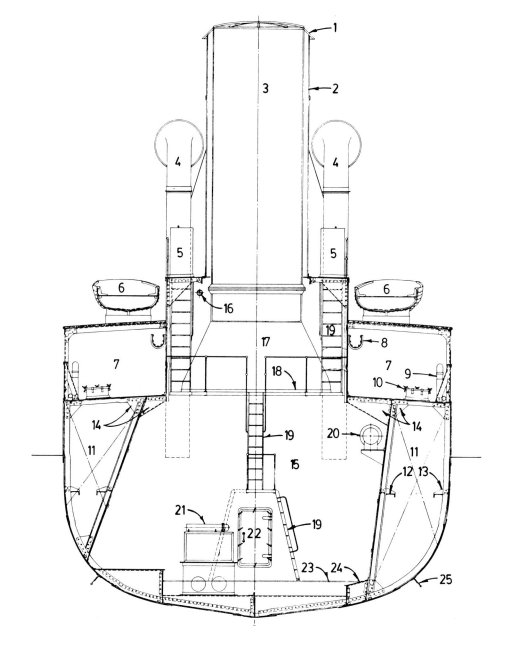

B3/14

B3/15 Cross section at '60' – looking aft

1. Pipe rail
2. 16ft dinghy
3. Davit
4. Rope reel
5. Upper deck
6. Depth charge stowage
7. Watertight manhole
8. Oil fuel tank
9. Stringer
10. Bulkhead stringer
11. Wash plate
12. Knees
13. Aft boiler room
14. 6in steam supply
15. Uptake
16. Scotch marine boiler
17. Exhaust steam feed water heater
18. Main feed pump
19. Sirocco fan
20. Oiltight gutterway
21. Grating
22. Boiler stool
23. Bilge keel

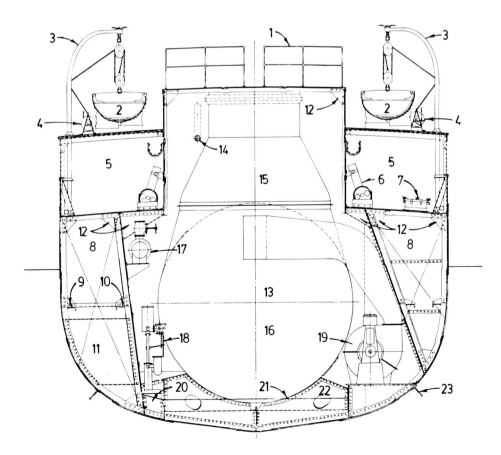

B3/15

B Internal hull

B3/16 Cross section at '64' – looking forward

1. Funnel cap
2. Funnel
3. Steam release pipe
4. Funnel guy
5. Boiler room vents
6. Pipe rail
7. 16ft dinghy
8. Boat davit
9. Rope reel
10. Life belt rack
11. Ladder
12. Air hatch
13. Upper deck
14. Depth charge stowage
15. Oiltight manhole
16. Oil fuel tank
17. Web plate
18. Knees
19. Stringer
20. Bulkhead stringer
21. Aft boiler room
22. Uptake
23. Rail
24. Platform
25. Boiler stay
26. Watertight door
27. Oil fuel pumping and heating unit
28. Vertical duplex transfer pump
29. Main feed pump
30. Oiltight gutterway
31. Bilge keel
32. Fireworks tank

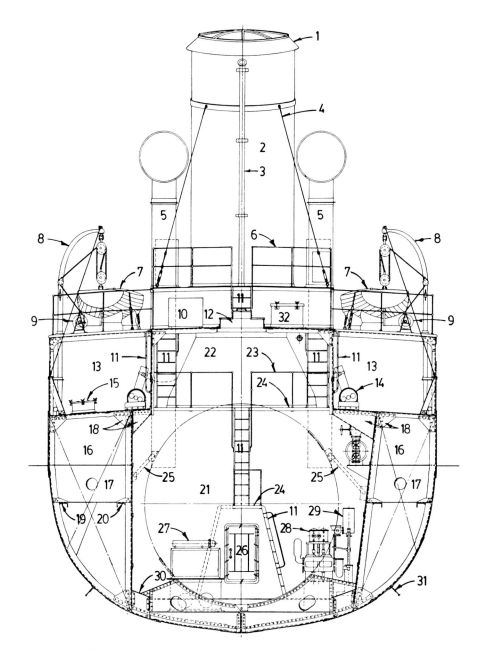

B3/16

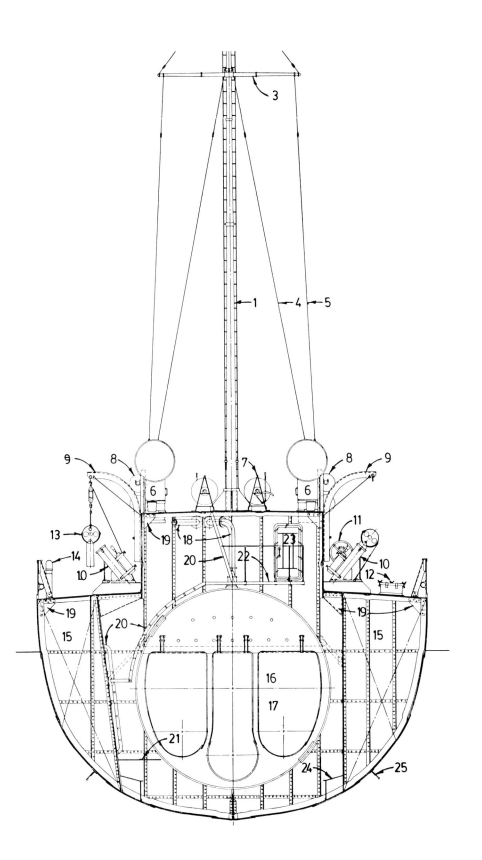

B3/17 *Cross section at '68' – looking aft*

1. Mainmast
2. Steaming light (electric)
3. Main yard
4. Mainmast shrouds
5. Main yard braces
6. Engine room vents
7. Purchase reel
8. Dan buoy and carrier/stanchion
9. Fixed davit over DC thrower
10. Depth charge thrower
11. 5in Downton pump
12. Oiltight manhole
13. Depth charge
14. Pipe vent
15. Oil fuel tank
16. Aft boiler room
17. Scotch marine boiler
18. 6in steam supply
19. Knee
20. Ladder
21. Grating
22. Platform
23. Watertight door
24. Oiltight gutterway
25. Bilge keel

B3/17

B Internal hull

B3/18 Cross section at '72' – looking aft

1. Dan buoy davit
2. Dan buoy
3. Dan buoy carrier/stanchion
4. Mushroom vent
5. Engine room skylight
6. Hinged gallows
7. Depth charge stowage
8. Degaussing cable
9. Engine room
10. Knee
11. 6in steam feed
12. Strut
13. Stringer
14. Reverse bar
15. Bilge keel
16. Engine bed
17. 2750hp Marine engine
18. Condenser
19. Seawater discharger
20. Vertical duplex general service pump
21. Feed water tanks
22. 14in circulating pump
23. Rail
24. Platform
25. Ladder
26. Monotype air pump
27. Oil tanks

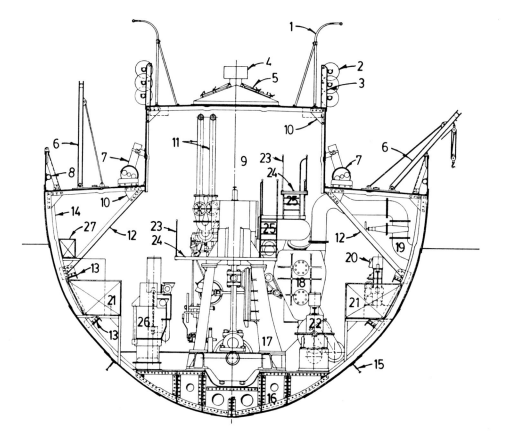

B3/18

B3/19 Cross section at '76' – looking aft

1. Dan buoy carrier/stanchion
2. Engine room skylight
3. Engine room vent
4. Depth charge stowage
5. Bulwark stay
6. Degaussing cable
7. Engine room
8. Knee
9. Reverse bar
10. Strut
11. Stringer
12. Engine bed
13. 2750hp Marine engine
14. Condenser
15. Seawater discharger
16. Vertical duplex bilge pump
17. Main injection valve
18. Rail
19. Platform
20. Pump for distiller plant

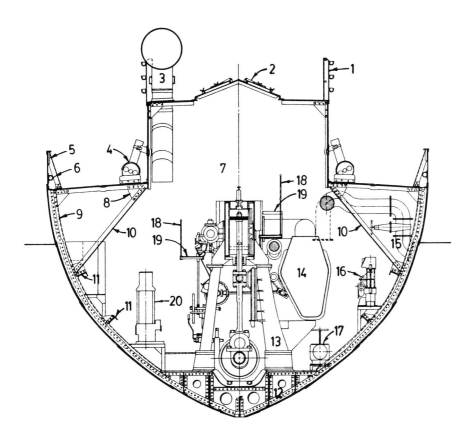

B3/19

B Internal hull

B3/20 Cross section at '80' – looking aft

1. After gun platform
2. Shelter
3. Lifebuoy
4. Fixed davit over DC thrower
5. Engine room vent
6. Mushroom vent
7. Engine room skylight
8. Wash deck locker
9. Kite/otter
10. Splinter protection plate
11. Depth charge cartridge box
12. Degaussing cable
13. Depth charge thrower
14. Spare otter board
15. Engine room
16. Knee
17. Stringer
18. Engine bed
19. Platform
20. Ladder
21. 2750hp Marine engine
22. Condenser
23. Fresh water and sanitary pumps
24. Work bench and vice

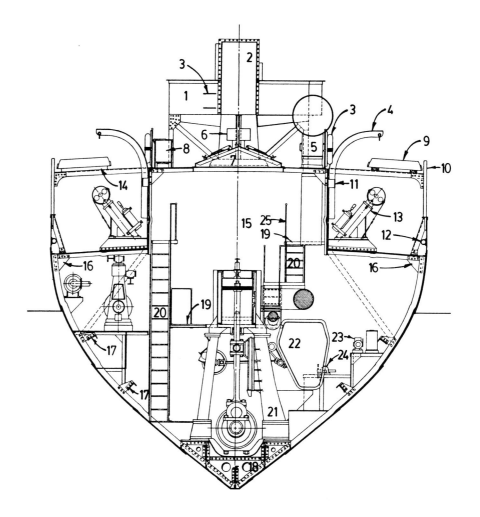

B3/20

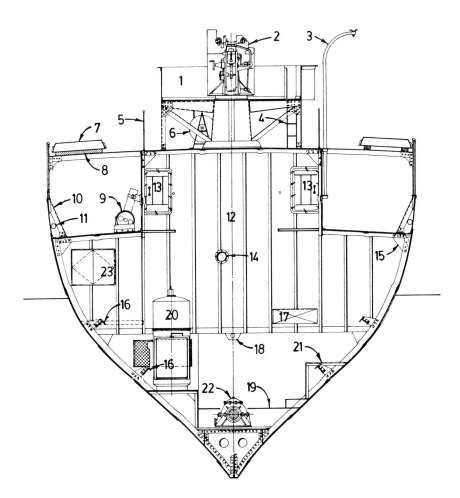

B3/21 Cross section at '84' – looking aft

1. After gun platform
2. 2pdr gun
3. Ammunition davit
4. Ladder
5. FSWR rail
6. Reel
7. Kite/otter
8. Spare otter board
9. Depth charge stowage
10. Bulwark stay
11. Degaussing cable
12. Engine room
13. Watertight door
14. Scuttle
15. Knee
16. Stringer
17. Opening in bulkhead (cover plate over)
18. Eye plate
19. Grating
20. Evaporator
21. Work bench
22. Thrust block
23. Switchboard

B3/21

B Internal hull

B3/22 Cross section at '88' – looking forward

1. After gun platform
2. 2pdr gun
3. Ammunition davit
4. Ladder
5. Reel
6. Kite/otter
7. Spare otter board
8. Pipe vent
9. Watertight door
10. Depth charge stowage
11. Bulwark stay
12. Degaussing cable
13. Officers' bathroom
14. Lobby
15. Ladder
16. Cabin No 4
17. Berth (drawers under)
18. Drawers
19. Wardrobe
20. Lobby
21. Scuttle
22. Cabin No 3
23. Hinged lavatory
24. Hinged desk
25. Engineers' store
26. Watertight hatch
27. Shelves
28. Shaft tunnel
29. Intermediate shaft

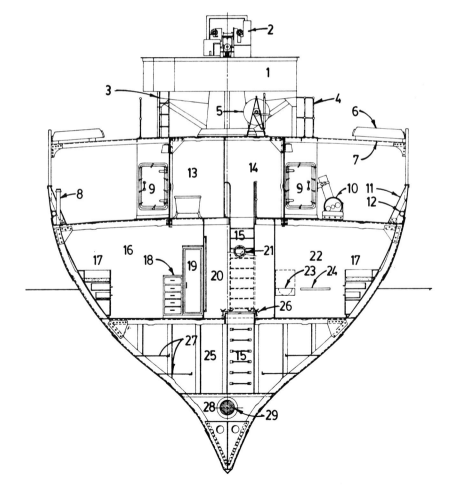

B3/22

B3/23 Cross section at '92' – looking forward

1. Lifebuoy
2. FSWR rail
3. Ready-use ammunition locker (for 2pdr gun)
4. Overtaking light
5. Handrail
6. Ladder
7. Depth charge stowage
8. Bulwark stay
9. Degaussing cable
10. Pipe vent
11. Cabin No 5
12. Girder
13. Pillar
14. Berth (drawers below)
15. Hinged desk
16. Hinged lavatory
17. Lobby
18. Ladder
19. Office
20. Cupboard
21. Eye plate
22. Engineers' store
23. Shelves
24. Tunnel shaft (intermediate shaft)

B3/24 Cross section at '96' – looking forward

1. Minesweeping winch
2. Bollard
3. Pipe vent
4. Bulwark stay
5. Degaussing cable
6. Girder
7. Knee
8. Pillar
9. Provision room
10. Loan clothing locker
11. Shelf
12. After peak
13. Stern tube

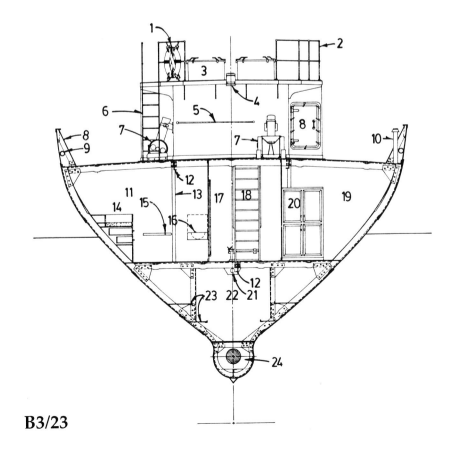

B3/23

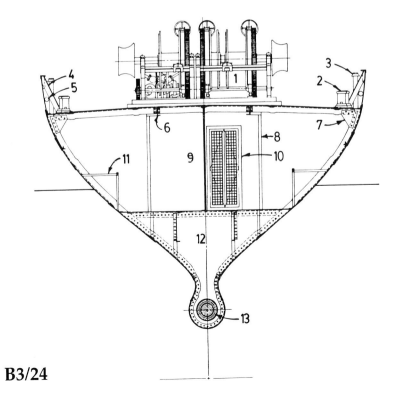

B3/24

B   Internal hull

B3/25   Cross section at '98' – looking aft

1. Minesweeping davit
2. Watertight hatch
3. Minesweeping float
4. Otter board
5. Degaussing cable
6. Pipe vent
7. Girder
8. Knee
9. Lobby
10. Ladder
11. No 1 store
12. Pillar
13. Bread locker
14. Shelf
15. Propeller bracket

B3/26   Cross section at '100' – looking aft

1. Minesweeping float
2. Otter board
3. Minesweeping davit
4. Watertight hatch
5. Knee
6. Steering gear flat and minesweeping store
7. Steering engine
8. Propeller bracket
9. Propeller

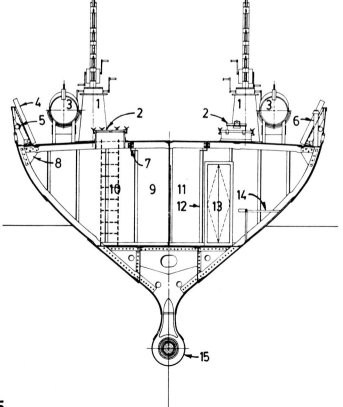

B3/25

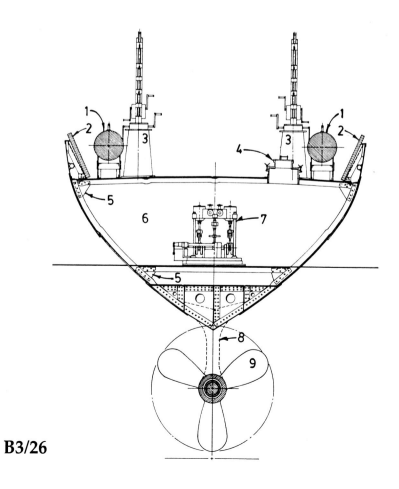

B3/26

B3/27 Cross section at '104' – looking aft

1. Smoke candle
2. Depth charge rails
3. Minesweeping davit
4. Bulwark stay
5. Degaussing cable
6. 12in plate beam
7. Web frame
8. Steering gear flat and minesweeping store
9. Emergency wheel
10. Rudder bearing
11. Rudder

B3/28 Cross section at '107' – looking aft

1. Ensign staff (portable)
2. Bulwark
3. Depth charge chute
4. Minesweeping fairlead
5. Steering gear flat and minesweeping store
6. Knee

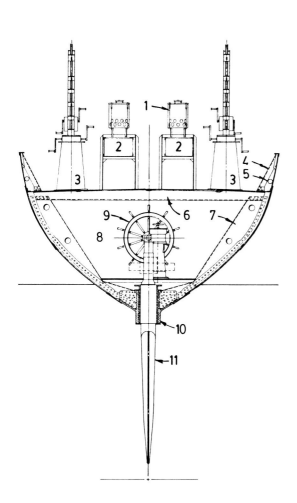

B3/27

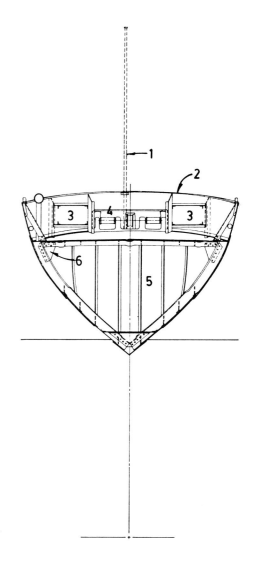

B3/28

C Construction

C1 HULL FRAMING (1/192 scale)

C1/1

C1/1 *Framing profile*

C1/2 *Framing plan*

Spaces
1. Store
2. Fore peak
3. Crew's messroom
4. Crew's accommodation
5. Crew's accommodation – port side
6. Crew's accommodation – starboard side
7. Chain locker and store
8. Asdic compartment
9. Fresh water tank
10. Side houses (P and S)
11. Reserve feed water tank
12. Magazine and spirit room
13. Magazine and fuel oil tanks
14. Forward boiler room
15. After boiler room
16. Engine room
17. Officers' accommodation
18. Engineers' store
19. Propeller shaft tunnel
20. Store rooms
21. After peak
22. Steering gear flat
23. Spirit room
24. 4in magazine
25. Oil fuel tank
26. 2pdr magazine
27. Forward boiler room casing
28. After boiler room casing
29. Engine room casing
30. Galley
31. Ventilator space
32. Funnel top

Framing members (oa open angle, ba bulb angle)

B.H.	Bulkhead
B.H.D.	Divisional bulkhead
B.H.P.	Bulkhead, port
B.H.P and S	Bulkhead, port and starboard
BMS 1	Beams 6in × 3in × .32 ba
BMS 2	Beams 5in × 3in × .31 oa
BMS 3	Beams 4in × 3in × .31 oa
BMS 4	Beams 4in × 3in × .38 oa
BMS 5	Beams 3½in × 6in × .40 oa
BMS CT	Cant beams 5in × 3in × .31 oa
BMS PL	12in plate beam
Compensation	9in × 3.25in × ½in ba fore and after compensation for cut frame at main injection valve
F.C.D.	Forecastle deck (of riveted construction)
FLS 1	Floors .30 flanged 4in (continuous across ship)
FLS 2	Floors .32 × 21in deep
FLS 3	Floors .32 × 21in deep flanged 4in

C1/2

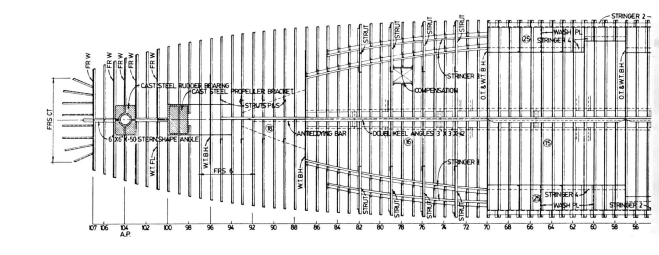

90

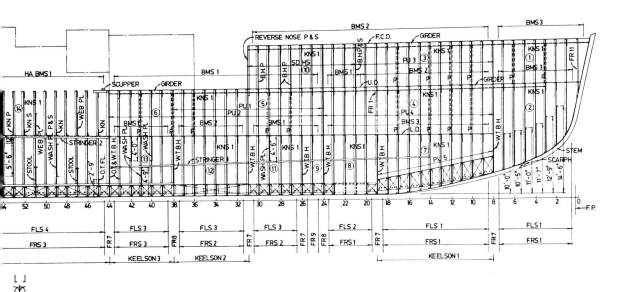

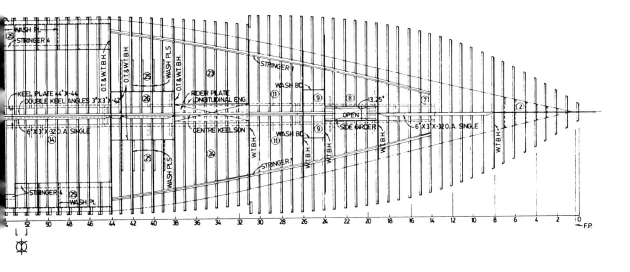

FLS 4	Floors .38 × 21in deep (except '45' flanged 4in) floors continuous except boiler stool floors
FLS 5	Floors .38 × 21in deep flanged 4in floors continuous except boiler stool floors
FLS 6	Floors .50
FLS 7	Floors .38 – intercostals .38 flanged 4in – vertical lugs 3in × 3in × .38
FLS 8	Floors .50 flanged 4in
FRS 1	Frames 6in × 3in × .36 oa
FRS 2	Frames 6in × 3in × .32 oa
FRS 3	Frames 6in × 3in × .32 oa cut in way of side bunker
FRS 4	Frames 6in × 3in × .32 oa except frames '82', '79', '76' and '73' which have reverse bars 6in × 3in × .32
FRS 5	Frames 6in × 3in × .32 oa except frames '101' and '107' – 9in × 3.5in × .40 ba
FRS 6	Boss frames 3.5in × 3.5in × .40
FR 7	Frame 3in × 3in × .38
FR 8	Frame 3.5in × 3.5in × .38 hooked
FR 9	Frame 6in × 3in × .32 oa
FR 10	Frame 3.5in × 3.5in × .50
FR 11	Frame 3.5in × 3.5in × .38
FR 12	Frame 3in × 2.5in × .26 oa
FR 13	Bulkhead framing – 3in × 2.5in × .26 oa
FRA	Asdic trunk framing 4in × 3in × .38*
FRC	Companion framing 4in × 3in × .38*
FRCT	Cant frames 6in × 3in × .32 oa
FR H	Hatch framing 4in × 3in × .38*
FR S	Skylight framing 4in × 3in × .38*
FR W	Web frame – see sections
G	Girder
HA BMS 1	Half beams 4in × 3in × .31 oa
HA BMS 2	Half beams 4in × 3in × .38 oa
HA BMS 3	Half beams 3in × 2.5in × .26 oa
HA BMS 4	Half beams 5in × 3in × .31
HA BMS 5	Half beams 6in × 3in × .32 ba
KEELSON 1	Centre keelson, intercostals .32, vertical angles 3in × 3in × .32
KEELSON 2	Centre keelson .32 in one piece (watertight) vertical angles 3in × 3in × .32 single
KEELSON 3	Centre keelson .32 fitted intercostally, vertical angles 3in × 3in × .32 single
KEELSON 4	Centre keelson, intercostal plates in boilerooms .38 – vertical lugs to floors 3in × 3in × .38 single – double lugs at boiler stools
KNS1	Beam knees 15in × .32
KNS2	Beam knees 18in × .32
KNS3	Beam knees 12in × .32

continued next page

C Construction

KNS4	Knees at foot 12in × .32 with 3in × 3in × .31 lugs*
KNS5	Beam knees 28in × .32 – 4in flange
KNS6	Outer beam knees 15in × .32
KNS7	Inner beam knees 18in × .32
KNS8	Inner beam knees 43in × .32 – 4in flange
KN	Beam knee
KN P	Knee (port only)
KN S	Knee (starboard only)
L.D.	Lower deck (of riveted construction)
O.T.B.H.	Oiltight bulkhead
O.T. FL.	Oiltight floor
O.T. and W.T.B.H.	Oiltight and watertight bulkhead
P	Pillar
PU1	Punch frames for joiner, port side (crew's accommodation)
PU2	Punch frames for joiner, starboard side (crew's accommodation)
PU3	Punch frames for joiner (crew's messroom)
PU4	Punch frames for joiner (crew's accommodation)
PU5	Punch floor flanges for 2in wood flooring
SCARPH	12in stem bar scarph – see detail
SCUPPER	Scupper and compensation – see detail
SD. HS.	Side houses, port and starboard
S.G. STG.	Framing for steering gear seating 3in × 3in × .38 oa*
STEM	Stem bar 7in × 1in flat
STOOL	Boiler stool
STRINGER 1	7in × 3.5in × .40 stringer, welded to frames
STRINGER 2	9in × 3.5in × .40 side stringer
STRINGER 3	9in × 3.5in × .40 ba side stringer
STRINGER 4	9in × 3.5in × .40 ba bulkhead stringer
STS	Stiffeners 3in × 2.5in × .26 oa
U.D.	Upper deck (of riveted construction)
WASH PL P	Wash plate, port side only
WASH PL P and S	Wash plate, port and starboard
WASH PL S	Wash plate, starboard side only
WEB PL	Web plate
W.T.B.H.	Watertight bulkhead
W.T. and O.T.B.H.	Watertight and oiltight bulkhead

C2 BEAMS AND CASING

C2/1 *Framing profile of the casing (1/192 scale)*

C2/2 *Framing plan of forecastle deck and casing (1/192 scale)*

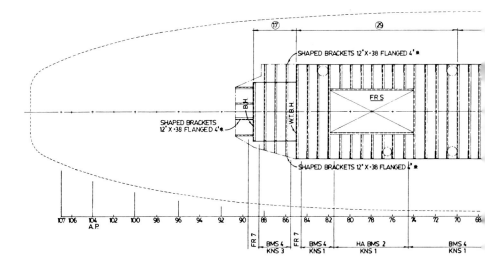

C2/2

C2/1

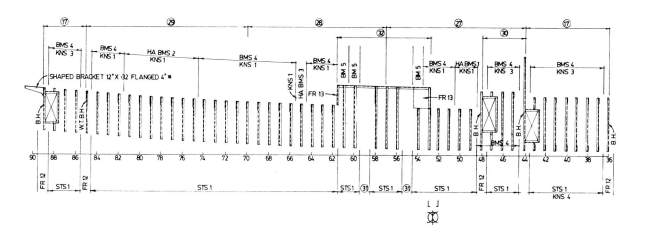
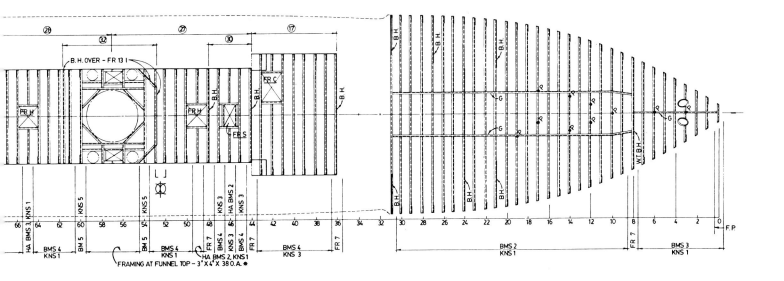

C Construction

C2/3 Upper deck framing plan (1/192 scale)

C2/4 Lower deck framing plan (1/192 scale)

see key on pages 90–92

C2/3

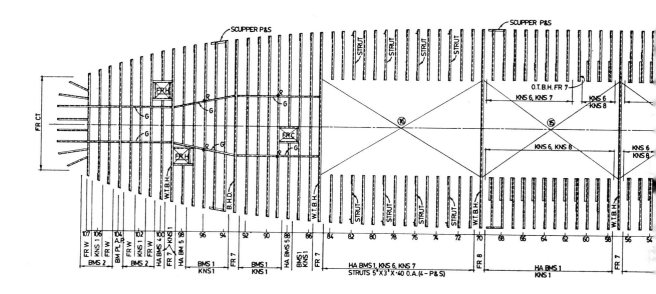

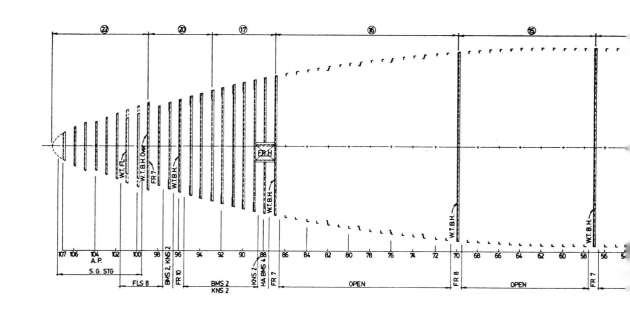

C2/4

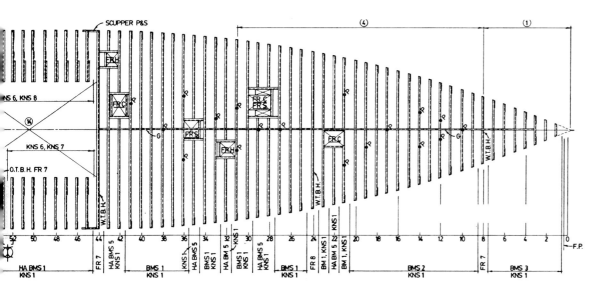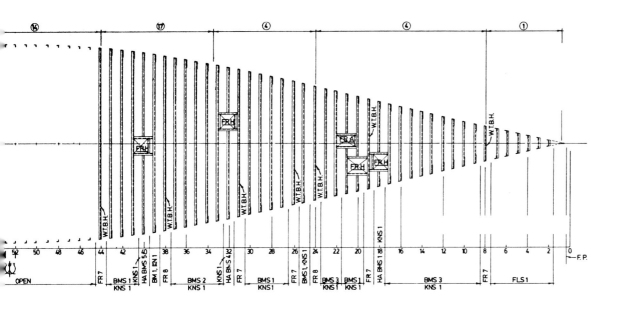

C Construction

C2/5 *Isometric view of casing frame (no scale)*

C2/6 *Isometric view of frames and beams (no scale)*

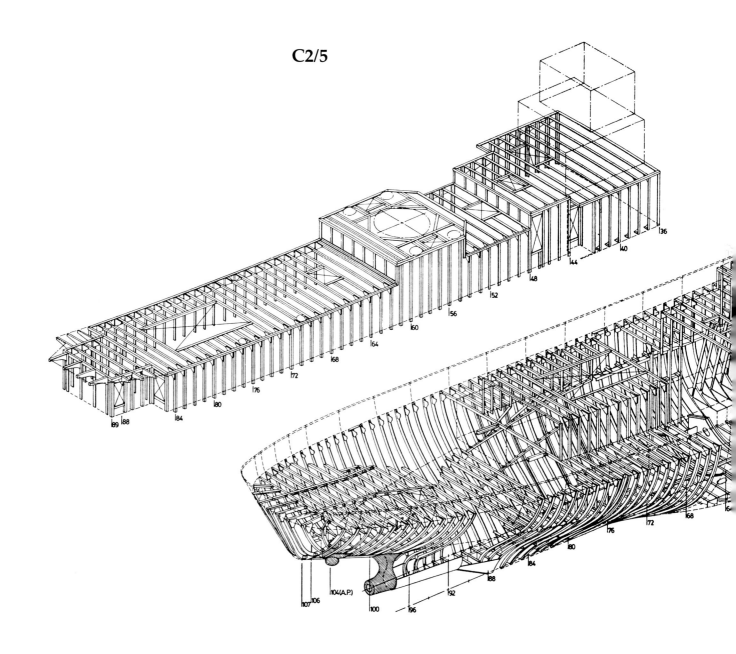

C2/5

C2/6

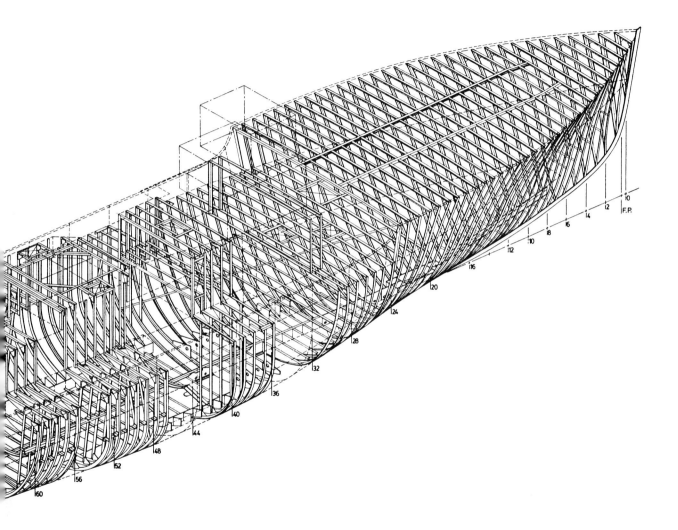

C Construction

C3 ISOMETRIC DETAILS (no scale)

Each isometric drawing shows construction of keel and floors at various points, identified by frame numbers.

C3/1 Frames 107–94

1. Cast steel rudder bearing
2. 6in × 6in × .50 stern shape angle
3. Cast steel propeller bracket
4. .50 floor
5. .40 bracket

C3/2 Frames 95–92

1. Seat for tunnel bearing
2. Boss frame 3.5in × 3.5in × .40
3. Frame 92

C3/3 Frames 91–88

1. 3in × 3in × .42 keel angles (double)
2. Anti-eddying bar
3. Floors .38 flanged 4in
4. Frame 88

C3/4 Frame 87–83

1. 3in × 3in × .42 keel angles (double)
2. 3in × 3in × .32 angle
3. Intercostal plate .32
4. Floors .50 (flanged 4in)
5. Frame 86

C3/5 Frames 78–75

1. 3in × 3in × .42 keel angles (double)
2. Intercostal plate .32 (flanged 4in)
3. Floor .50 (flanged 4in)
4. Floor .50 (flanged 4in)
5. Intercostal plate .32

C3/6 Frames 70–65

1. 3in × 3in × .42 keel angles (double)
2. Intercostal plate .32
3. Frame 68
4. Intercostal .38
5. 6in × 3in × .32 oa single
6. 3in × 3in × .42 angle
7. Floor (.38 boiler stool)
8. Floor .38 (flanged 4in)
9. Bracket
10. Stiffener 5in × 3in × .31 oa

C3/7 Frames 62–58

1. 3in × 3in × .42 keel angles (double)
2. Frame 61
3. Intercostal plate .38
4. Floor .38 (flanged 4in)
5. 6in × 3in × .32 oa single
6. Intercostal plate .38
7. Floor .38 (flanged 4in)
8. Stiffener 5in × 3in × .31 oa
9. Bracket

C3/8 Frames 43–39

1. 3in × 3in × .42 keel angles (double)
2. Frame 42

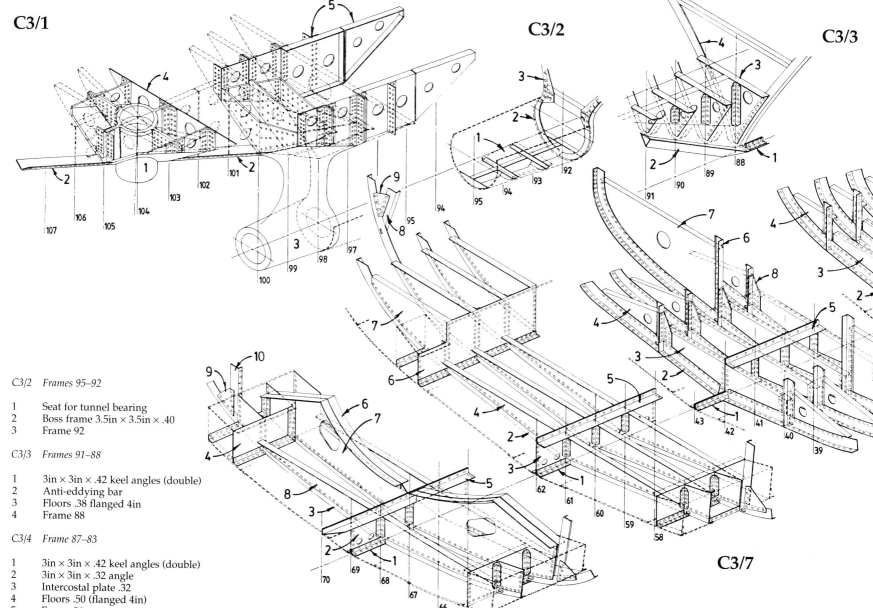

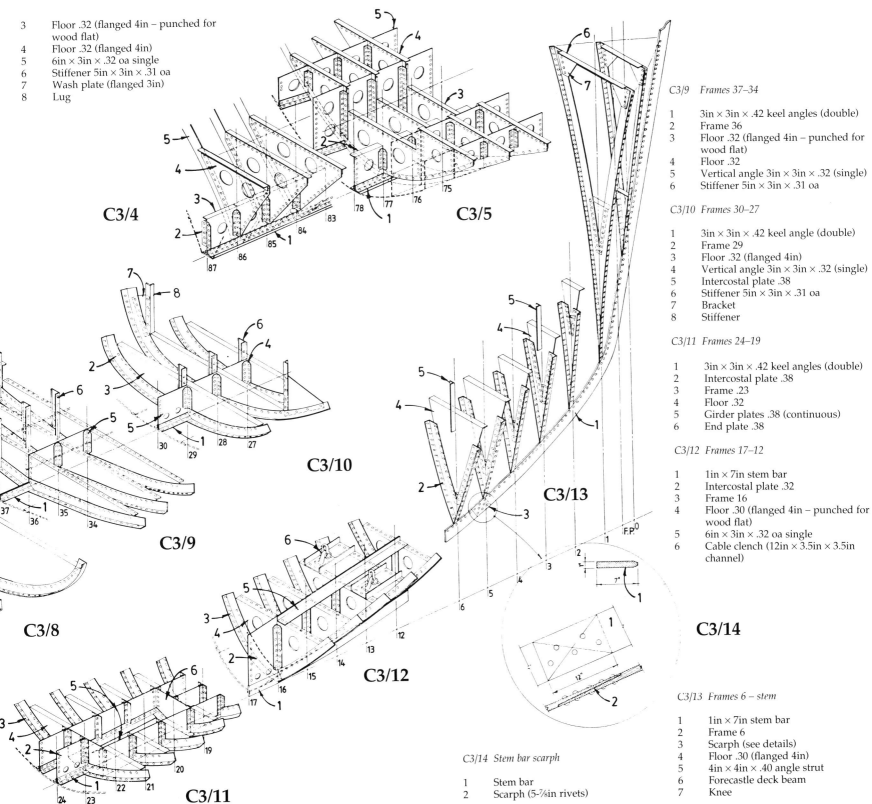

3 Floor .32 (flanged 4in – punched for wood flat)
4 Floor .32 (flanged 4in)
5 6in × 3in × .32 oa single
6 Stiffener 5in × 3in × .31 oa
7 Wash plate (flanged 3in)
8 Lug

C3/9 *Frames 37–34*

1 3in × 3in × .42 keel angles (double)
2 Frame 36
3 Floor .32 (flanged 4in – punched for wood flat)
4 Floor .32
5 Vertical angle 3in × 3in × .32 (single)
6 Stiffener 5in × 3in × .31 oa

C3/10 *Frames 30–27*

1 3in × 3in × .42 keel angle (double)
2 Frame 29
3 Floor .32 (flanged 4in)
4 Vertical angle 3in × 3in × .32 (single)
5 Intercostal plate .38
6 Stiffener 5in × 3in × .31 oa
7 Bracket
8 Stiffener

C3/11 *Frames 24–19*

1 3in × 3in × .42 keel angles (double)
2 Intercostal plate .38
3 Frame .23
4 Floor .32
5 Girder plates .38 (continuous)
6 End plate .38

C3/12 *Frames 17–12*

1 1in × 7in stem bar
2 Intercostal plate .32
3 Frame 16
4 Floor .30 (flanged 4in – punched for wood flat)
5 6in × 3in × .32 oa single
6 Cable clench (12in × 3.5in × 3.5in channel)

C3/14 *Stem bar scarph*

1 Stem bar
2 Scarph (5-⅞in rivets)

C3/13 *Frames 6 – stem*

1 1in × 7in stem bar
2 Frame 6
3 Scarph (see details)
4 Floor .30 (flanged 4in)
5 4in × 4in × .40 angle strut
6 Forecastle deck beam
7 Knee

C Construction

C4 BILGE KEELS (1/16 scale)

C4/1 11in bilge keel

1. Shell
2. 6in × 4in × ⅜in tee bar
3. 10 in × ⅜in bulb plate

C4/2 22in bilge keel

1. Shell
2. 6in × 4in × ⅜in tee bar
3. 10in × ⅜in bulb plate
4. ⅜in plate
5. Shaped bracket
6. 2in × 2in angle

C5 SCUPPER COMPENSATION

C5/1 Elevation (1/16 scale)

C5/2 Section (1/16 scale)

1. Scupper
2. 3in × 3in × .34 oa stringer bar
3. Deck plating
4. 3in × 3in × .34 compensation bar
5. Frame

C5/3 Isometric view (no scale)

1. Scupper
2. 3in × 3in × .34 oa stringer bar
4. 3in × 3in × .34 compensation bar
5. Frame

C6 WASHPORT

C6/1 Elevation (1/32 scale)

C6/2 Section (1/32 scale)

1. 5in × 3in × .31 ba rail bar – hooked
2. Bulwark stay
3. Shell
4. Washport door
5. Hinge
6. Deck plating
7. Stringer bar
8. Joggle in door

C6/3 Isometric view (no scale)

1. 5in × 3in × .31 ba rail bar – hooked
3. Shell
4. Washport door
5. Hinge
6. Deck plating
7. Stringer bar
8. Joggle in door

C4/1

C4/2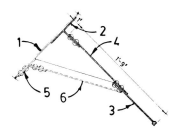

C5/2 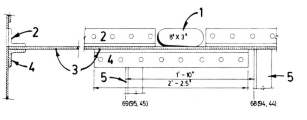  **C5/1**

C5/3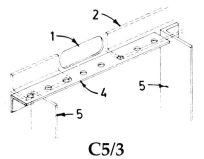

C6/1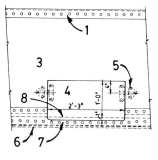

C6/2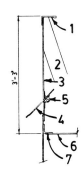

C6/3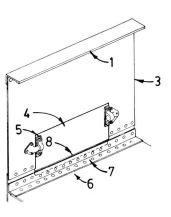

C7/1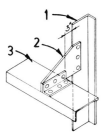

C7/2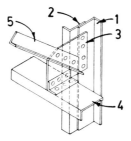

C7/3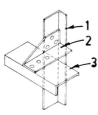

C7/4

C7 STRINGERS (no scale)

C7/1 Lower stringer in engine room

1 Frame
2 .32 plate (with 3in × 3in × .32 lug)
3 9in × 3.5in × .40 ba stringer

C7/2 Upper stringer in engine room at reverse frame

1 Frame
2 6in × 3in × .32 reverse bar
3 .32 plate (3in × 3in × .32 lug)
4 9in × 3.5in × .40 ba stringer
5 5in × 3in × .40 ba strut

C7/3 Stringer in fuel oil tanks

1 Frame
2 5in × 5in × .32 lug
3 9in × 3.5in × .40 stringer

C7/4 Stringer forward of frame 44

1 7in × 3.5in × .40 stringer (weld to frame)
2 Frame

C8 BULWARK STAY

C8/1 Elevation (1/32 scale)

1 Deck plating
2 Shell
3 Stringer
4 5in × 3in × .31 oa bulwark stay
5 5in × 5in × .40 oa lug
6 3in × 3in × .30 oa lug
7 5in × 3in × .31 ba rail bar – hooked

C8/2 Isometric view (no scale)

1 Deck plating
2 Shell
3 Stringer
4 5in × 3in × .31 oa bulwark stay
5 5in × 5in × .40 oa lug
6 3in × 3in × .30 oa lug
7 5in × 3in × .31 ba rail bar – hooked
8 Deck beam
9 Knee
10 Frame

C6/4 Washport door hinge – elevation, section and plan (1/8 scale)

1 Washport door
2 Bulwark
3 2in × ¼in flat steel
4 Spindle
5 Socket
6 ⅛in nb bushing

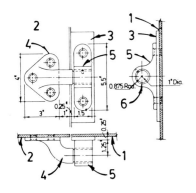

C6/4

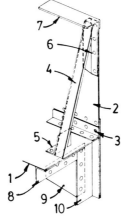

C8/1

C8/2

C Construction

C9   ISOMETRIC VIEW OF FRAMES (no scale)

C10 ISOMETRIC VIEW OF KEEL AND FLOORS (no scale)

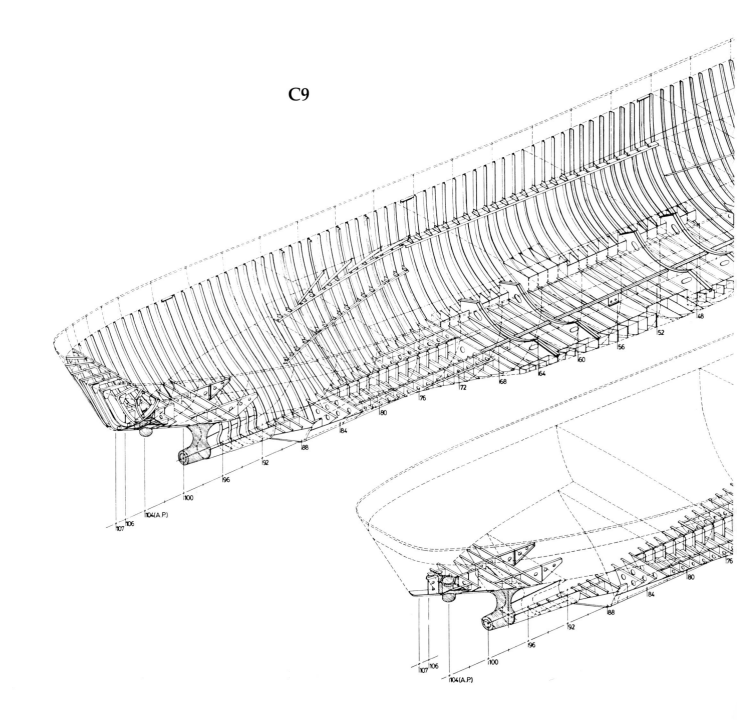

C9

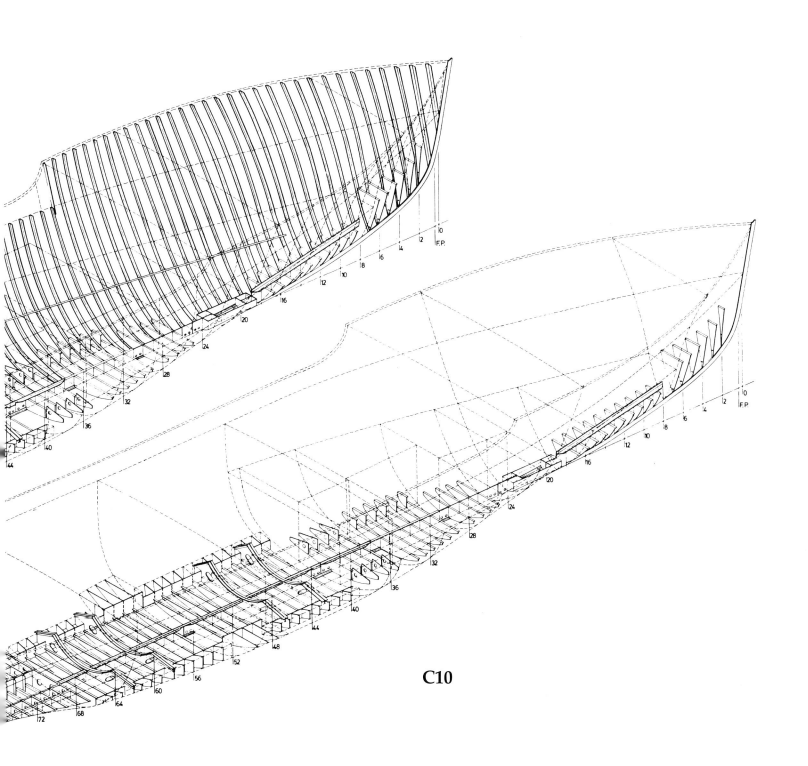

C10

C Construction

C11 STERN FRAMING (no scale)

1. Cast steel rudder bearing
2. Rudder
3. Cast steel propeller bracket
4. Propeller
5. Cant frames
6. Beam (5in × 3in × .31 oa)
7. Web frames
8. Frame 98 (6in × 3in × .32 oa)
9. Stern shape angle (6in × 6in × .50)
10. Floor
11. Girder
12. Line of upper deck
13. Line of bulwark
14. Bulwark stay
15. Knee

C12 RUDDER (1/48 scale)

Particulars of rudder
Rudder area – 85.5sq ft
Speed – 16kts
CG of area abaft CL of stock = 2.86ft aft of CL of stock
Area of rudder abaft CL of stock = 63.6sq ft = 74.4% of total area
CG of total rudder area = 1.86ft aft of CL of stock
Torque = 321in tons (going ahead)
Torque = 349in tons (going astern)

C12/1 Cross section
C12/2 Longitudinal section
C12/3 Aft elevation
C12/4 Plan
C12/5 Section at 6ft 6in
C12/6 Section at 3ft 6in

C13/1

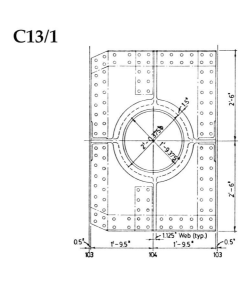

C13/3

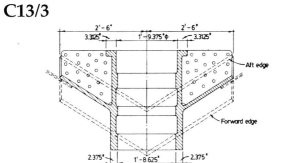

C13/2

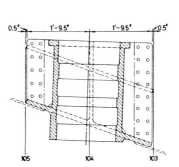

C13/4

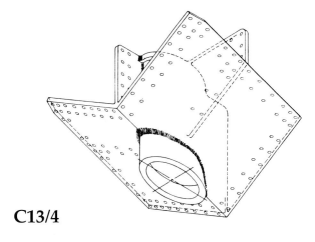

C13 CAST STEEL RUDDER BEARING

C13/1 Plan (1/32 scale)

C13/2 Side section (1/32 scale)

C13/3 End section (1/32 scale)

C13/4 Isometric view from below (no scale)

C13/5 Isometric view from above (no scale)

C13/6 Detail of bearing (1/16 scale)

1. Gland (gunmetal)
2. ¾in dia countersunk bolts
3. Bearing
4. Packing
5. Lignum vitae
6. Bearing ring
7. Cast steel bearing
8. Bearing ring
9. Brass cage
10. 1in dia bolts

C13/7 Gland detail (1/32 scale)

C13/8 Bearing ring (1/32 scale)

C13/5

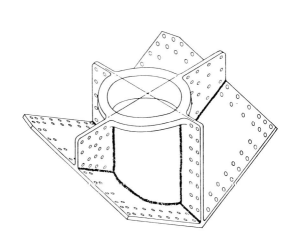

C13/6

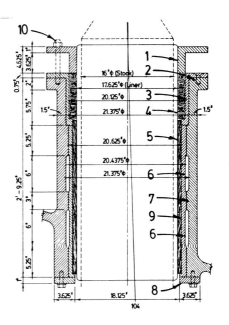

C13/7

C13/8

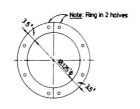

C Construction

C14   SHELL EXPANSION (1/192 scale)

Plate sizes

Strake 'G'
1 13ft 9in × .28
2 15ft 5in × 58in × 55in × .28
3 14ft 1in × 13ft 7in × 62in × .28
4 10ft 10.5in × 10ft 4.5in × 62.5in × .28
5 13ft 3in × 12ft 9in × 62in × .28
6 11ft 9in × 11ft 3in × 57.5in × .50

Strake 'F'
1 10ft 0in × 42in × .28
2 12ft 2in × 41in × .26
3 13ft 10.5in × 37in × .26
4 17ft 2.5in × 34.5in × .26
5 16ft 10in × 34.5in × .26
6 16ft 10in × 34.5in × .26
7 22ft 4in × 35in × .26
8 16ft 10in 34.5in × .26
9 15ft 0in × 34.5in × .26
10 15ft 0in × 34.5in × .26
11 17ft 0in × 36.25in × .28
12 17ft 9in × 17ft 6in × 39.5in × .28
13 18ft 3in × 18ft 0in × 40in × .28
14 17ft 3in × 16ft 9in × 38.25in × .30

Strake 'E'
1 7ft 6in × 7ft 0in × 80in × .26
2 9ft 2in × 9ft 8in × 75in × .26
3 10ft 9in × 73.5in × .26
4 11ft 11.5in × 70in × .26
5 11ft 10in × 66in × .30
6 11ft 11.5in × 11ft 8.5in × 62.75in × .34
7 11ft 11in × 11ft 8in × 62.25in × .38
8 12ft 1in × 11ft 9in × 63.75in × .42
9 17ft 4.5in × 1.5in × 65.5in × .42
10 22ft 8in × 65.5in × .42
11 15ft 4in × 64.75in × .42
12 15ft 5in × 65.25in × .42
13 17ft 8in × 17ft 5in × 67.75in × .38
14 19ft 11.5in × 19ft 5.5in × 68.5in × .34
15 16ft 3in × 15ft 9in × 68.75in × .30
16 13ft 2in × 12ft 8in × 62.75in × .30

Strake 'D'
1 8ft 6in × .26
2 9ft 6in × 9ft 0in × 9ft 2in × .26
3 11ft 0.5in × 10ft 6.5in × 86in × .26
4 12ft 4in × 11ft 10in × 84.5in × .28
5 13ft 10in × 80.75in × 77.25in × .32
6 11ft 9in × 75.75in × 73.75in × .36
7 13ft 9in × 73in × .40
8 13ft 11in × 75.75in × .40
9 13ft 8in × 78in × 76in × .40
10 13ft 4.5in × 78in × .40
11 13ft 7in × 78in × .40
12 13ft 10in × 13ft 7in × 77.5in × .40
13 17ft 8in × 17ft 5in × 78in × .38
14 17ft 10in × 17ft 6in × 76.75in × .34
15 17ft 10in × 72.5in × 69.5in × .32
16 18ft 8in × 18ft 2in × 67.5in × .32

Key to outboard fittings

A   2in storm valve, port
B   4in storm valve, port
C   4in storm valve, port
D   2in storm valve, port
E   Transfer pump discharge, starboard
F   Sea valve, port
G   General service pump discharge, starboard
H   Main discharge, port
I   Bilge pump discharge, port
J   Main injection, port
K   Distiller pump discharge, starboard
L   2in storm valve, starboard
M   2in storm valve, port
N   3in convex rubbing piece (typical), port and starboard
S   Strut at bulwark

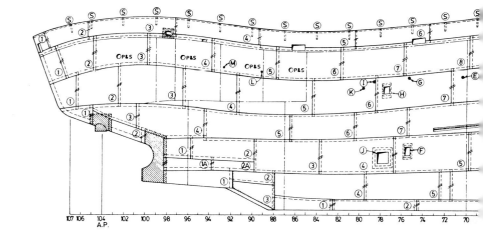

C14

Strake 'C'
1. 7ft 3in × 48in × 15in × .50
2. 7ft 9in × 7ft 6in × 36.5in × .50
3. 8ft 10in × 46in × 8in × .40
4. 13ft 2in × 12ft 11in × 62.5in × .30
5. 16ft 1in × 15ft 10in × 62.75in × .30
6. 12ft 1in × 63.75in × .34
7. 13ft 7in × 65in × .38
8. 13ft 8in × 68.5in × .38
9. 13ft 7in × 71.5in × .38
10. 11ft 9in × 72in × .38
11. 13ft 6.5in × 72in × .38
12. 13ft 8in × 71in × .38
13. 15ft 9.5in × 15ft 6.5in × 68.75in × .38
14. 13ft 10.5in × 13ft 7.5in × 67in × .38
15. 17ft 8in × 17ft 5in × 64.5in × .34
16. 17ft 6.5in × 61in × 58in × .32
17. 11ft 3in × 58in × .32

Strake 'B'
1. 5ft 9in × 54in × .50
1A. 9ft 4in × 45in × 39in × .50
2. 12ft 3in × 51in × .30
2A. 8ft 0in × 36in × .36
3. 12ft 0in × 69in × .34
4. 13ft 8.5in × 71.5in × .36
5. 13ft 8in × 73.75in × .38
6. 11ft 7.5in × 76.5in × .38
7. 13ft 4.5in × 77.75in × .38
8. 15ft 2.25in × 77.25in × .38
9. 11ft 7in × 77.75in × .38
10. 13ft 8in × 69in × .38
11. 13ft 8.5in × 54.5in × 48.5in × .38
12. 18ft 2in × 44.5in × 38.5in × .38

Strake 'A'
1. 12ft 6in × 41in × 35in × .50
2. 7ft 8in × 29in × 25in × .50
3. 7ft 9in × 53in × 24in × .44
4. 16ft 3.5in × 61in × 55in × .40
5. 13ft 6in × 69in × 62.5in × .38 spacer
6. 20ft 9in × 73.5in × .38 spacer
7. 18ft 10.5in × 74in × .38 spacer
8. 20ft 8.5in × 74in × .38 spacer
9. 18ft 10.5in × 71.5in × 65.5in × .38
10. 13ft 6in × 59.25in × 53.25in × .38
11. 8ft 1in × 45in × 39in × .38
12. 11ft 6in × 67in × 48in × .38
13. 20ft 0in × 69in × 10in × .38

Note: strake 'A' starboard side only is shown

Keel
1. 10ft 0in × 56in × 50in × .50
2. 14ft 8.5in × 44.5in × .44
3. 16ft 6in × 44.5in × .44
4. 20ft 2.5in × 44.5in × .44
5. 18ft 4.5in × 44.5in × .44
6. 18ft 4.5in × 44.5in × .44
7. 14ft 8.5in × 44.5in × .44
8. 16ft 0in × 50in × .44
9. 7ft 8in × 30in × .44

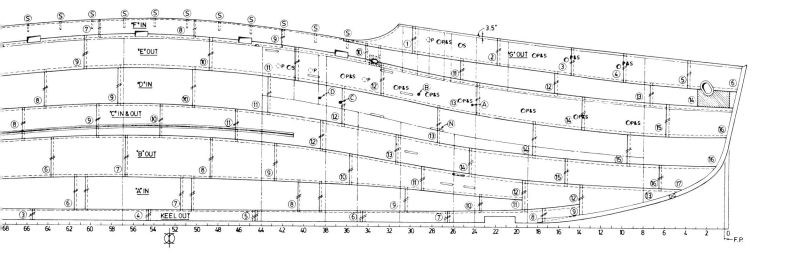

D Machinery

D1 ENGINE ROOMS AND BOILER ROOMS

D1/1 Plan of lower level (1/96 scale)

1. Save all
2. Oil fuel tank
3. Forward boiler room
4. Aft boiler room
5. Galley stove oil tank
6. Wash plate
7. Ladder
8. Boiler stools
9. Oiltight gutterway
10. Oiltight manhole
11. Platform over
12. Boiler room vents over
13. Watertight door
14. Engine room
15. Skylight over
16. Stringer
17. Engineers' store
18. Reverse frames

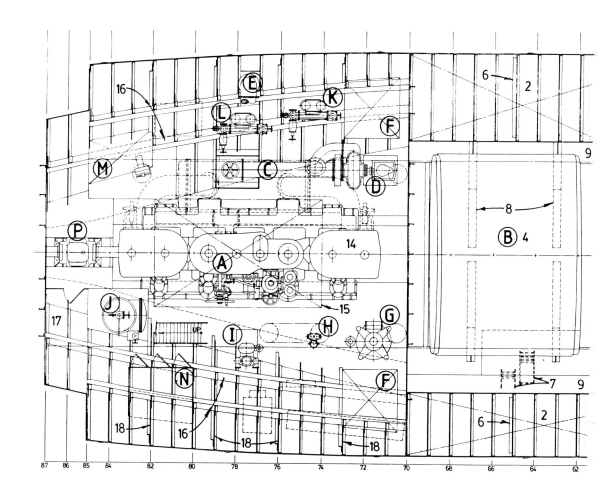

D1/1

D1/2 Elevation of starboard side (1/96 scale)

1. Accommodation
2. Engineers' store
3. Engine room
4. Stringer
5. Ladder
6. Grating
7. Reverse frames
8. Grating
9. Aft boiler room
10. Forward boiler room
11. Boiler stools
12. Boiler stays
13. Ladders
14. Grating

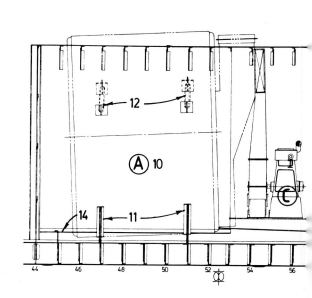

D1/2

108

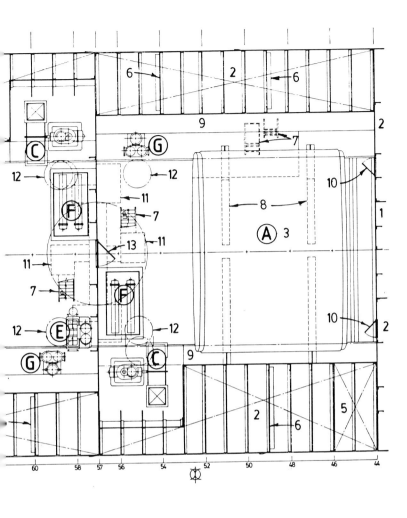
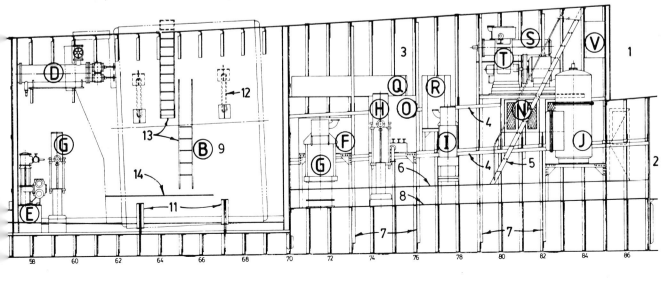

Engine room equipment

- A 2750hp Marine engine – 18.5in × 31in × 38.5in × 38.5in × 30in stroke × 225lb
- B Condenser
- C Main injection valve
- D 14in circulating pump and engine
- E Seawater discharger
- F Feed water tanks (port and starboard) (Hotwell tanks)
- G Monotype air pump – 24in pump × 12in cylinder × 15in stroke
- H Stand-by feed pump – 8in pump × 10.5in cylinder × 22in stroke
- I Pump for distiller plant – 6.5in steam cylinder × 10in stroke – 8in diameter circulating pump – 5in diameter fresh water pump – 3.75in diameter brine pump
- J Evaporator – 25 tons per 24 hours
- K Vertical duplex general service pump – 6in pump × 6in cylinder × 6in stroke
- L Vertical duplex bilge pump – 6in pump × 6in cylinder × 6in stroke
- M Chequer plate work bench and vice
- N Lockers
- O Feed water filter – twin clear type – 60,000lb per hour capacity
- P Thrust block (Michell type)
- Q Oil tanks
- R Oil tank
- S Fresh water distiller – 5600 gals per 24 hours
- T 15kW, 110 volt electric generator and engine
- U Fresh water and sanitary pumps
- V Switchboard

Boiler room equipment

- A Scotch marine boiler (forward)
- B Scotch marine boiler (aft)
- C 35in Sirocco fan directly coupled to engine (port and starboard)
- D Exhaust steam feed water heater (port and starboard) 80sq ft heating surface
- E Vertical duplex transfer pump – 4in pump × 4in cylinder × 5in stroke
- F Oil fuel pumping and heating unit, duplicate unit installation for Smith's liquid fuel system
- G Main feed pump (port and starboard) – 6in pump × 8.5in cylinder × 18in stroke

D Machinery

D1/3 *Plan of upper level (1/96 scale)*

1. Accommodation
2. Oil fuel tank
3. Web plate
4. Forward boiler room
5. Aft boiler room
6. Boiler stay
7. 6in steam supply
8. Knee
9. Line of uptake
10. Ladder
11. Platform
12. Engine room
13. Skylight over
14. Engine room vent over
15. Watertight door

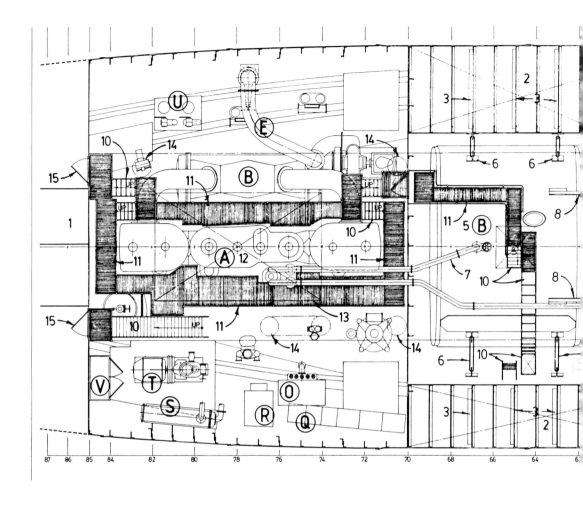

D1/4 *Elevation of port side (1/96 scale)*

1. Forward boiler room
2. Aft boiler room
3. Boiler stools
4. Oiltight floor
5. Boiler stays
6. Ladders
7. Grating
8. Engine room
9. Accommodation
10. Stringer
11. Reverse frames

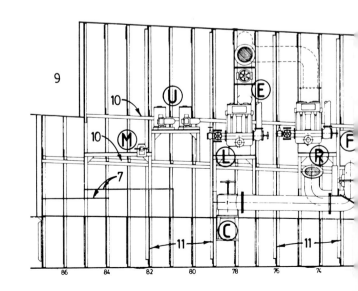

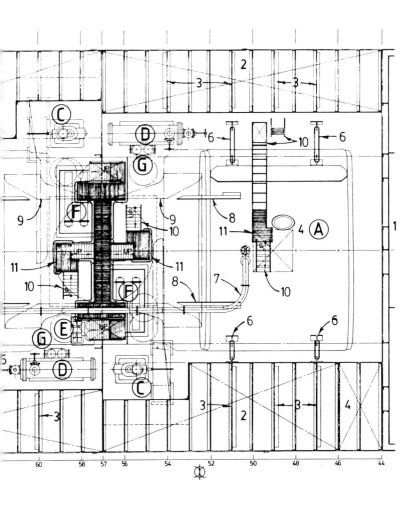
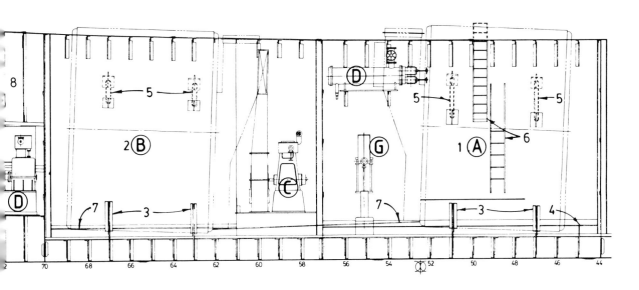

111

D Machinery

D2 2750hp MARINE ENGINE (1/48 scale)

D2/1 *Section through aft low pressure cylinder looking forward*

D2/2 *Port elevation*

D2/3 *Starboard elevation*

D2/4 *Section through high pressure cylinder looking aft*

D2/5 *Plan*

D2/6 *Plan of engine base*

1 Engine base (bed plate)
2 Column
3 Condenser
4 Metal cover
5 Gauges
6 Feed lubricator
7 Guard rail
8 Thrust shaft coupling
9 Main bearings
10 Crank webs
11 Packing gland
12 Piston rod
13 Cross head and connecting rod upper bearing
14 Connecting rod
15 Connecting rod lower bearing (crank pin)
16 Cross head guide
17 Slipper
18 Relief valve
19 Crankshaft centreline
20 Eccentric rod
21 Valve spindle
22 Eccentric (sheave and strap)
23 Radius link
24 Drag links
25 Cut-off adjustment block
26 Reversing arm
27 Reversing shaft
28 Reversing wheel
29 Drive chain
30 Reversing lever
31 Reversing engine
32 Steam to reversing engine
33 Exhaust from reversing engine to condenser
34 Worm gear

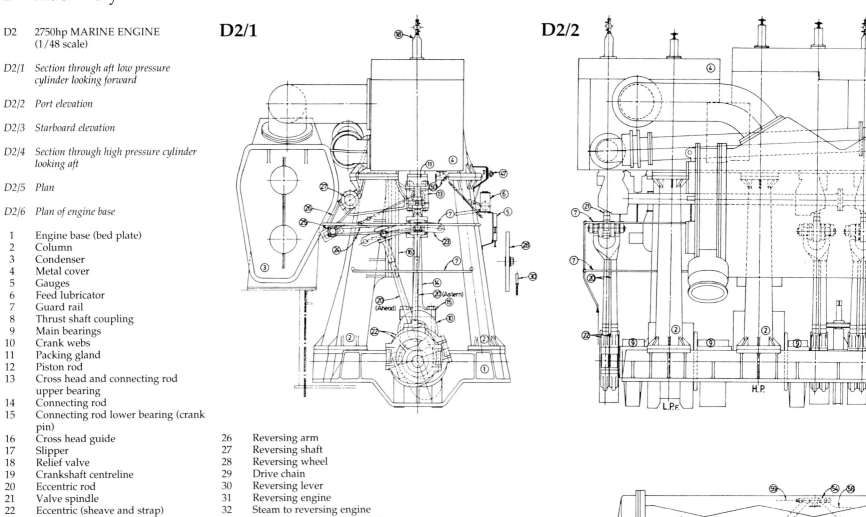

D2/1 D2/2

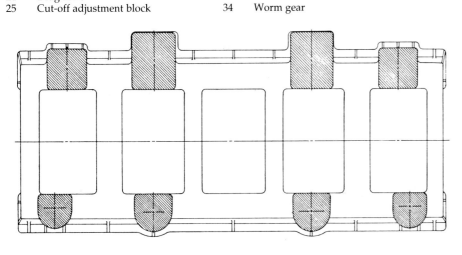

D2/6

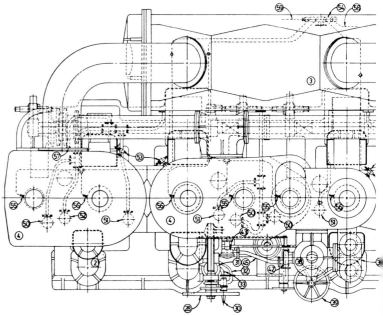

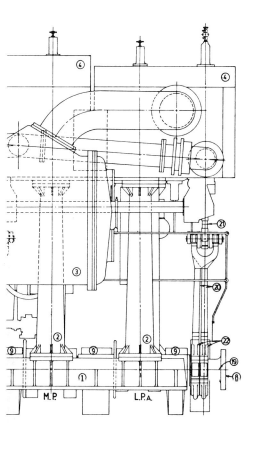
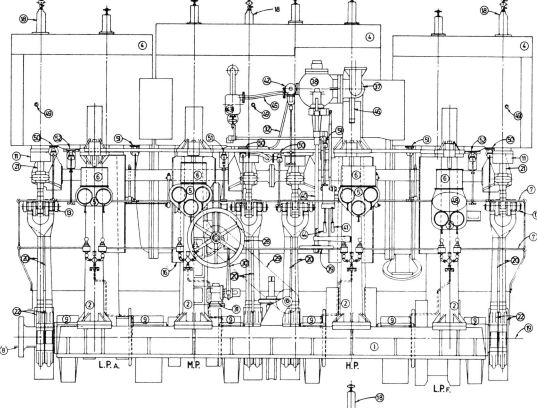
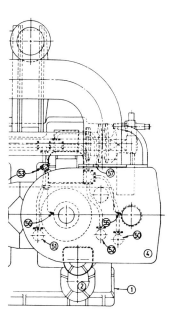
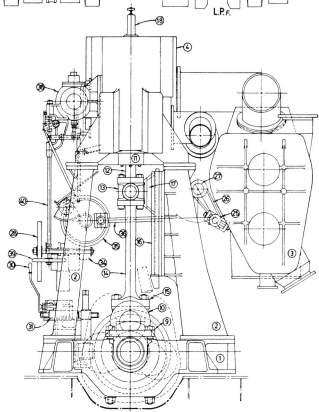

35	Reversing gear
36	Reversing gear rod
37	Branch piece (steam)
38	Throttle valve
39	Throttle wheel
40	Throttle wheel shaft
41	Throttle lever
42	Two-part stop valve
43	Starting valve (pass over valve)
44	Starting valve lever
45	Steam to starting valve
46	Branch piece support
47	Shaft for mechanical lubricators
48	Engine builder's plaque
49	Chest pressure gauge connection
50	Chest drain valve
51	Cylinder drain valve
52	Cylinder port drain valve
53	Indicator cock
54	Collector piece
55	Globe valve valve spindle drain
56	Globe valve piston rod drain
57	Exhaust belt drain
58	Extra feed from tanks to condenser
59	Evaporator coil (drains to condenser)

D3   BOILERS (1/48 scale)

D3/1   *Longitudinal section of forward Scotch marine boiler A and A1 and aft Scotch marine boiler B and B1*

D3/2   *Front half elevation*

D3/3   *Half section A–A*

D3/4   *Rear half elevation*

1   1 9/16 in shell plate
2   1 9/16 in head plate
3   15/16 in head plate
4   Centre furnace
5   Side furnace
6   Centre furnace opening
7   Side furnace opening
8   Splice plate
9   Manhole opening (aft boiler)
10   Manhole opening (forward boiler)
11   12in × 16in opening
12   Stay rods
13   Stay tubes and plain tubes
14   Stay tubes
15   Back stays
16   Side stays
17   Steam supply (aft boiler)
18   Steam supply (forward boiler)

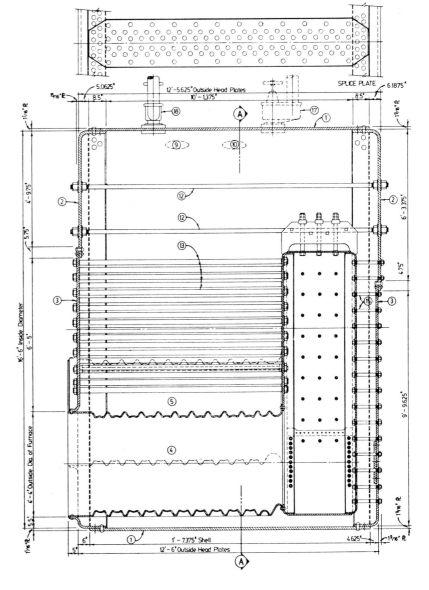

D3/1

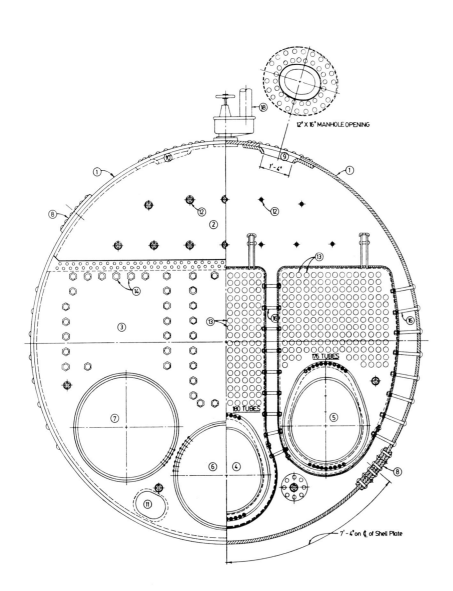

D3/2

D3/3

114

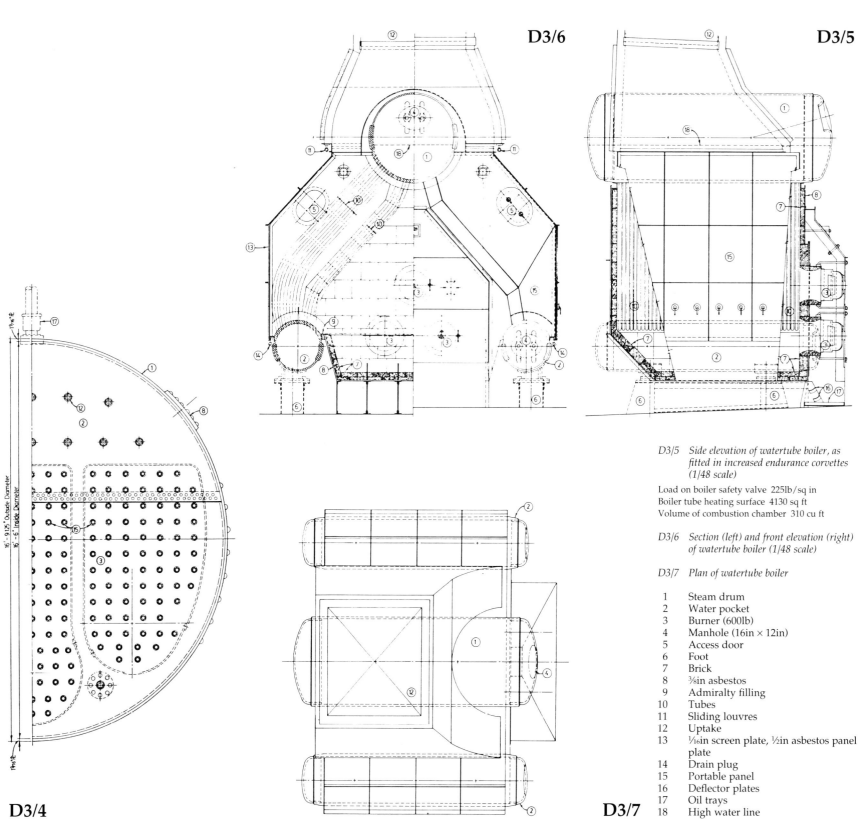

D3/5 Side elevation of watertube boiler, as fitted in increased endurance corvettes (1/48 scale)

Load on boiler safety valve 225lb/sq in
Boiler tube heating surface 4130 sq ft
Volume of combustion chamber 310 cu ft

D3/6 Section (left) and front elevation (right) of watertube boiler (1/48 scale)

D3/7 Plan of watertube boiler

1 Steam drum
2 Water pocket
3 Burner (600lb)
4 Manhole (16in × 12in)
5 Access door
6 Foot
7 Brick
8 ⅜in asbestos
9 Admiralty filling
10 Tubes
11 Sliding louvres
12 Uptake
13 1/16in screen plate, ½in asbestos panel plate
14 Drain plug
15 Portable panel
16 Deflector plates
17 Oil trays
18 High water line

D Machinery

D3/8 Profile sketch showing arrangement of watertube boilers (1/96 scale)

1. Funnel
2. High casing
3. Casing top
4. Upper deck
5. Reserve feed water tank
6. Forward boiler
7. Aft boiler
8. Uptake

D4 CONDENSER (1/48 scale)

D4/1 Plan

D4/2 Section

D4/3 Forward elevation

D4/4 Section

D4/5 Section at support plates

1. Shell
2. Shell top
3. Forward door
4. Aft door
5. Upper support frame
6. Lower support frame
7. Perforated plate
8. Manhole
9. 2in square bar
10. 1¾in square bar
11. Cylinder drain
12. Separator drain
13. Cabin heating drain
14. Air pump suction
15. Hand hole
16. Vacuum gauge connection
17. Relief valve connection
18. Silent blow off connection

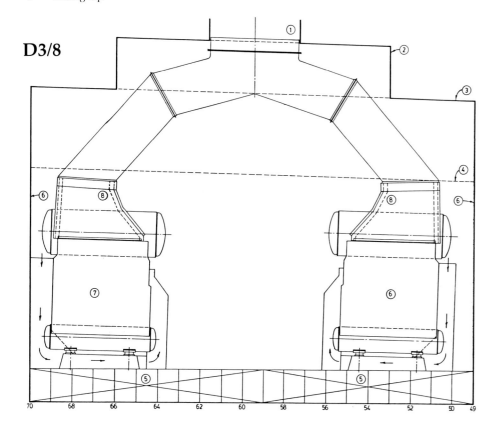

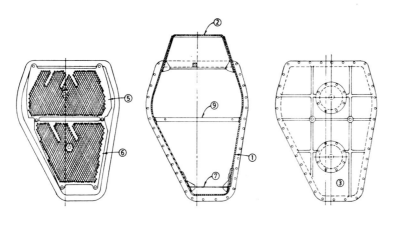

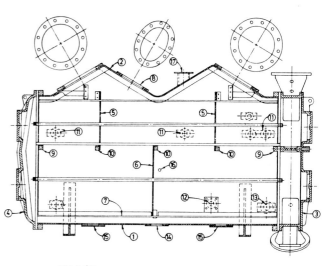

D5 DISTILLER PUMP (1/48 scale)

D5/1 End elevation

D5/2 Side elevation

D5/3 Plan

D6 FRESH WATER DISTILLER (1/48 scale)

D6/1 End elevation

D6/2 Side elevation

D6/3 Plan

D7 ELECTRIC GENERATOR (1/48 scale)

D7/1 Aft elevation

D7/2 Starboard elevation

D7/3 Plan

D8 AIR PUMP (1/48 scale)

Weir C.1. Monotype – based on drawings by HMC Dockyard, Halifax NS, 23 February 1943. Built by Morton Engineering and Dry Dock Co Ltd, Quebec PQ.

D8/1 Port elevation

D8/2 Section looking aft

D8/3 Plan

D5/2

D5/1

D5/3

D7/1

D7/2

D7/3

D6/2

D6/3

D6/1

D8/1

D8/2

D8/3

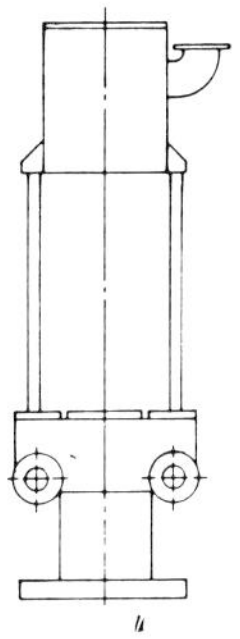

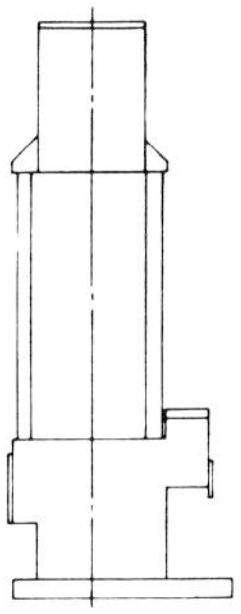

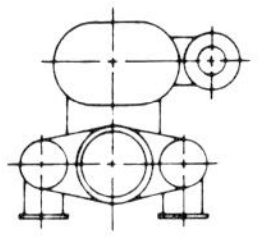

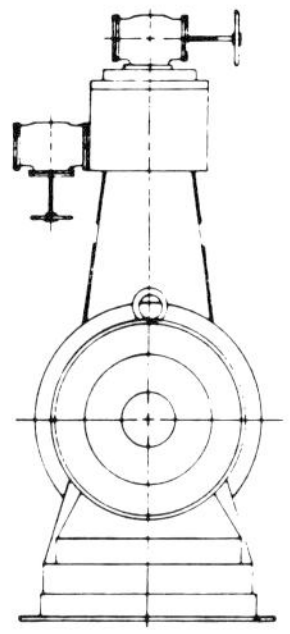

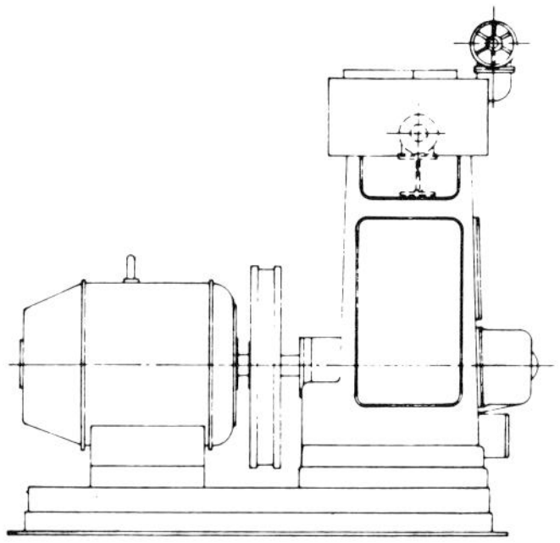

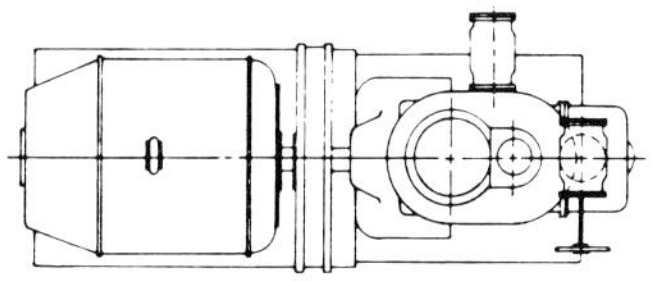

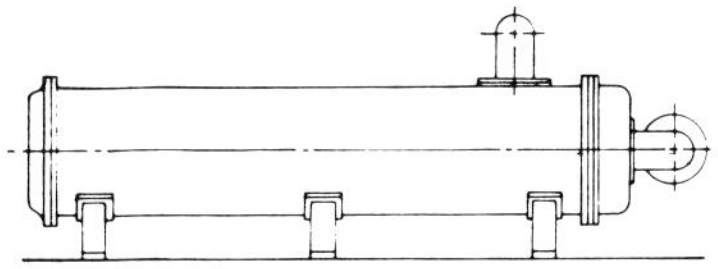

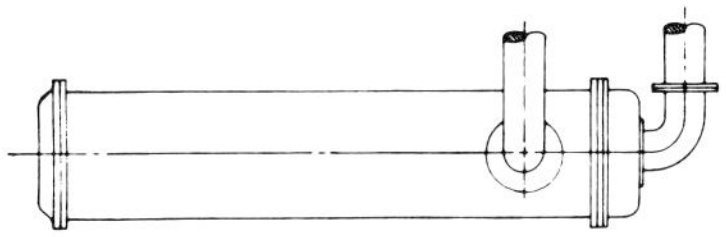

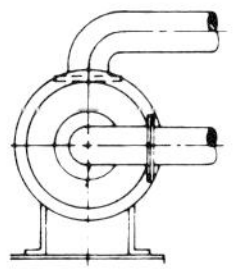

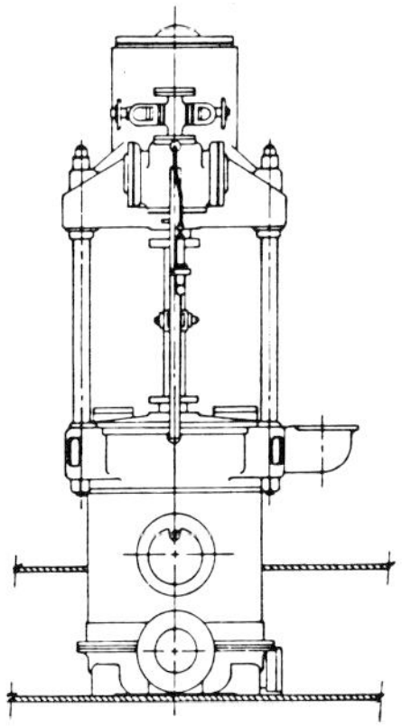

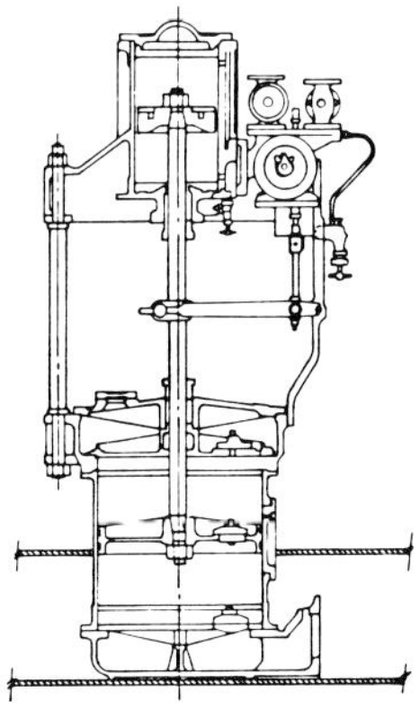

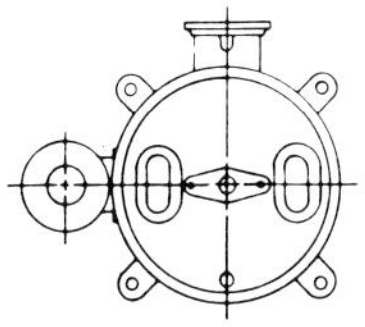

D Machinery

D9   MAIN INJECTION VALVE AND 14in MAIN CIRCULATING PUMP AND ENGINE

D9/1   *Starboard elevation (1/48 scale)*

1   1¼in steam
2   2in return
3   Pump
4   Engine
5   Feed to condenser
6   Main injection valve
7   Engine base
8   Engine seat
9   Engine room floors
10   Shell

D9/2   *Forward elevation (1/48 scale)*

1   1¼in steam
2   2in return
3   Engine
4   Pump
5   Engine base
6   Engine seat

D9/3   *Plan (1/48 scale)*

1   1¼in steam
2   2in return
3   Pump
4   Engine
5   Feed to condenser
6   Main injection valve

D9/4   *Aft elevation – main injection valve (1/48 scale)*

1   Main injection valve
2   9in × 3½in × .50 BA fore and after
3   6in × 6in lug
4   Shell
5   .43 doubling
6   Engine seat
7   Engine room floor

D10   STAND AND FEED PUMP (1/48 scale)

Weir cast iron feed pump, based on drawings by Peacock Brothers Ltd, Engineers, Montreal.

D10/1   *Elevation*

D10/2   *Section*

D10/3   *Plan*

D11   25-TON EVAPORATOR (1/48 scale)

D11/1   *Forward elevation*

D11/2   *Side elevation*

D11/3   *Plan*

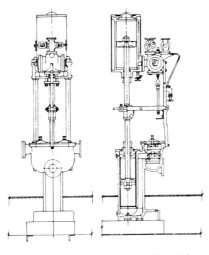

D9/1

D9/2

D9/3

D9/4

D10/1   D10/2

D10/3

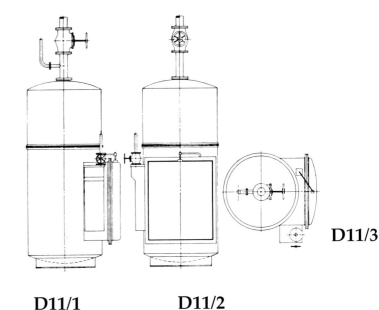

D11/1   D11/2   D11/3

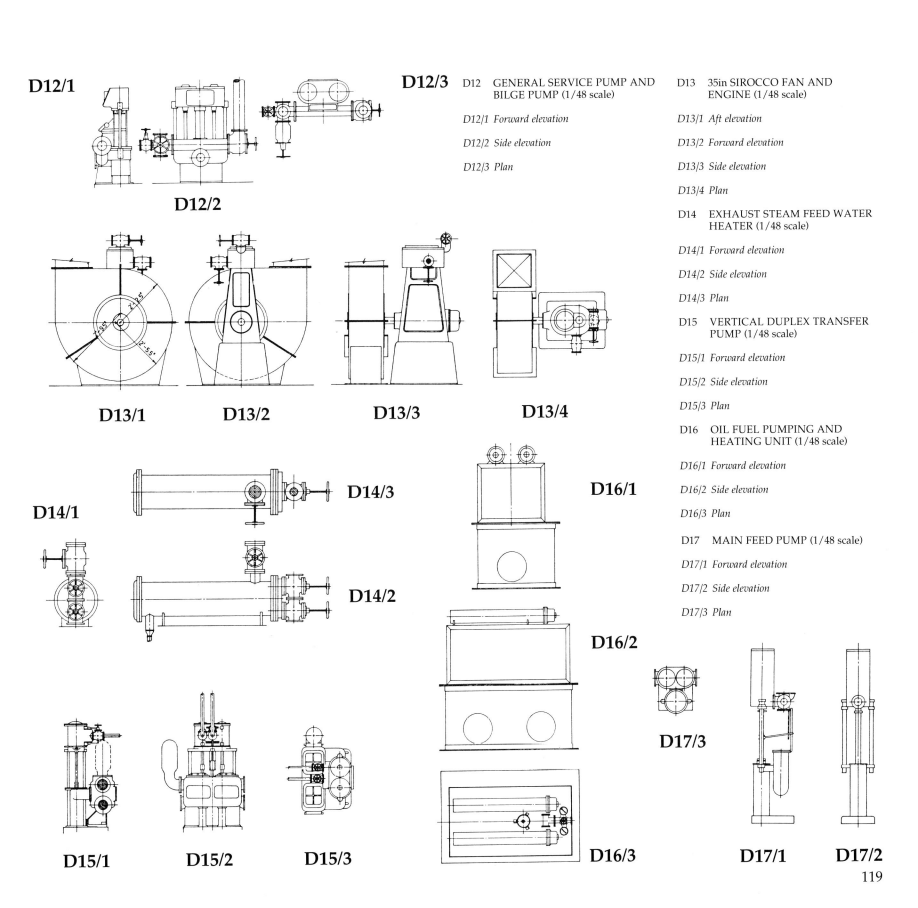

D12 GENERAL SERVICE PUMP AND BILGE PUMP (1/48 scale)
D12/1 Forward elevation
D12/2 Side elevation
D12/3 Plan

D13 35in SIROCCO FAN AND ENGINE (1/48 scale)
D13/1 Aft elevation
D13/2 Forward elevation
D13/3 Side elevation
D13/4 Plan

D14 EXHAUST STEAM FEED WATER HEATER (1/48 scale)
D14/1 Forward elevation
D14/2 Side elevation
D14/3 Plan

D15 VERTICAL DUPLEX TRANSFER PUMP (1/48 scale)
D15/1 Forward elevation
D15/2 Side elevation
D15/3 Plan

D16 OIL FUEL PUMPING AND HEATING UNIT (1/48 scale)
D16/1 Forward elevation
D16/2 Side elevation
D16/3 Plan

D17 MAIN FEED PUMP (1/48 scale)
D17/1 Forward elevation
D17/2 Side elevation
D17/3 Plan

D Machinery

D18 PROPELLER ASSEMBLY
(1/48 scale)

D18/1 Propeller shaft assembly

D18/2 Stern tube and gland

D18/3 Tunnel bearing

D18/4 Michell type thrust block

Thrust block design data
Shaft diameter	10½in
Ihp	2750
Rpm	185
Thrust load	42,000lb
Thrust surface	224sq in
Thrust pressure	188lb per sq in
Total fore and aft clearance	0.030in approx
Clearance on diameter of journal	0.17in approx
Cooling surface of coils	3.125sq ft

1 Casing top
2 Casing bottom
3 Stops
4 Cover
5 Thrust shoes
6 Thrust pads
7 Journals
8 Cooling coil door
9 Coiling coil
10 Couplings
11 Oil scraper
12 Filler plug
13 Wiper

14 Liners
15 Fitted bolts (0.75in dia)
16 Babbit
17 Oil gauge
18 Plug for oil drain
19 Gasket
20 Gasket

D18/5 Tail end spanner

D18/6 Propeller

D18/7 Cowl

D19 CAST STEEL PROPELLER BRACKET

D19/1 Forward elevation (1/48 scale)

D19/2 Starboard elevation (1/48 scale)

D19/3 Aft elevation (1/48 scale)

D19/4 Plan (1/48 scale)

D19/5 Middle palm looking forward (1/48 scale)

D19/6 Section at 'A' (1/48 scale)

D19/7 Section at 'B' (1/48 scale)

D19/8 Isometric view from aft (no scale)

D19/9 Isometric view from forward (no scale)

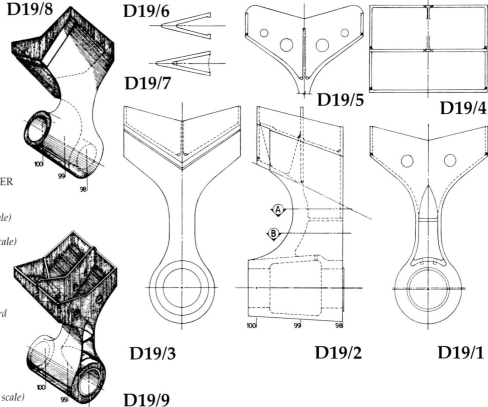

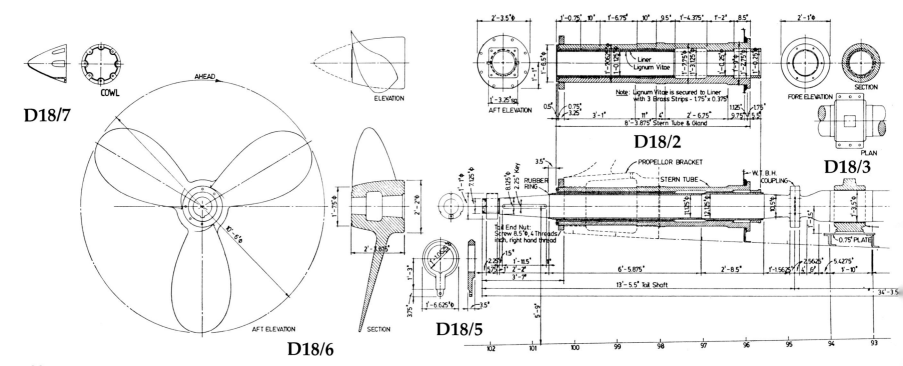

D20 WILSON-PIRRIE TYPE STEERING
      GEAR (1/48 scale)

Particulars of steering engine

Diameter of cylinders	7in
Stroke of pistons	7in
Working pressure	100lb
Hydraulic test pressure	400lb
Revolutions, hard over to hard over (for 70 degrees)	81
Load exerted on quadrant teeth by engine	0.7 tons
Working angle of gear, mid to hard over	35 degrees

D20/1 Forward elevation

D20/2 Aft elevation

D20/3 Starboard elevation

D20/4 Plan

1 Emergency wheel
2 Rudder head
3 Quadrant
4 Bronze friction washer
5 Friction clutch
6 Handwheel for operating friction clutch
7 Handwheel for local control
8 2in steam
9 2½ exhaust
10 Telemotor receiving cylinder
11 Handgear quadrant
12 Engine base plate
13 Handgear standard
14 Engine cylinders
15 Piston rods
16 Anti-shock springs

D21 BRIDGE TRANSMITTER FOR
      HYDRAULIC TELEMOTOR
      (1/16 scale)

Donkin & Co Ltd, Engineers, Walker Gate,
Newcastle-upon-Tyne, 10 March 1939.

D21/1 Starboard elevation

D21/2 Aft elevation

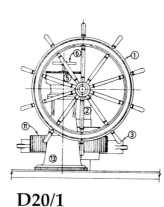
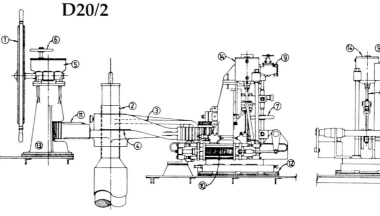
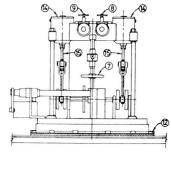
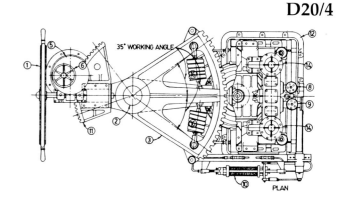
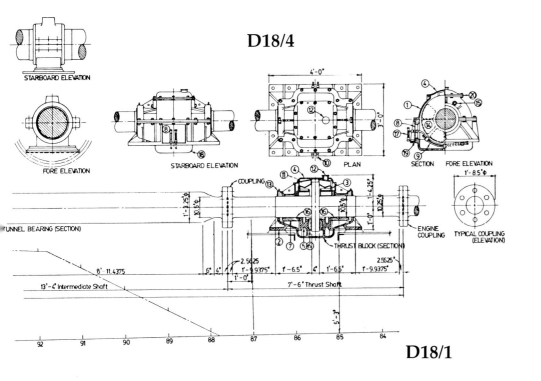
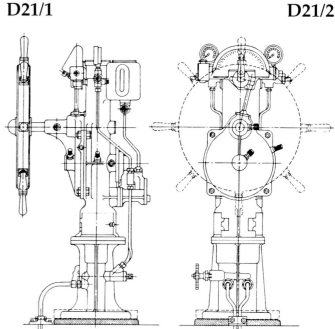

D Machinery

D22 PUMPING AND VENTING (1/192 scale)

D22/1 Pumping and venting profile

D22/2 Pumping and venting plan

1. 2in GI air pipe to chain locker (port)
2. 10in cowl vent to seamen's mess (CL)
3. 10in CV to seamen's mess (stbd)
4. 2in GI air pipe to fore peak (stbd)
5. 9in scuttles to upper and lower decks
6. 8in mushroom vent to seamen's mess
7. 4in MV to asdic compartment
8. 4in MV to fresh water tank (port)
9. 4in MV to reserve feed water tank (port)
10. 4in MV to asdic compartment
11. 4in MV to fresh water tank (stbd)
12. 4in MV to reserve feed water tank (stbd)
13. 6in MV to washplace
14. 4in MV to WCs
15. Skylights to CPOs' and POs' mess deck
16. 6in MV to provision issue room
17. 4in MV to refrigerated room
18. 4in MV to canteen
19. 6in MV to POs' washplace
20. 4in MV to POs' WC
21. Ward room skylight
22. 6in MV to ward room
23. 3in GI air pipe to spirit room
24. 6in MV to pantry
25. 4in MV to officers' store
26. Hatch
27. 6in MV to cabin No 1
28. 3in GI air pipe to shell room
29. 6in MV to cabin No 2
30. 6in GI air pipe to oil fuel tanks (port and starboard)
31. 3in GI air pipe to galley stove oil tank
32. Oiltight manhole to galley stove oil tank (filling)
33. Oiltight manhole to oil fuel tanks (filling) (port and starboard)
34. 6in GI air pipe to oil fuel tanks (port and starboard)
35. 4in MV to engineers' store
36. 4in MV to cabin No 4
37. 4in MV to cabin No 5
38. 4in MV to provision room
39. 3in GI air pipe to engineers' store
40. 4in MV exhaust to steering gear flat
41. Hatch to steering gear flat
42. Hatch to lobby
43. 4in MV to cabin No 3
44. 4in MV to engineers' store
45. 4in MV to office
46. 4in MV to No 1 store
47. 3in GI air pipe to engineers' store
48. 4in CV to steering gear flat
49. 9in diameter galley range funnel
50. Galley skylight
51. 8in MV to galley
52. Air hatch
53. 24in CV to forward boiler room
54. 24in CV to aft boiler room
55. 24in CV to forward boiler room
56. 24in CV to aft boiler room
57. Air hatch
58. 20in CV to engine room
59. 20in CV to engine room
60. 20in CV to engine room
61. 20in CV to engine room
62. Engine room skylight
63. 12in MV to engine room skylight
64. 4in MV to officers' bath
65. 4in MV to lobby
66. Watertight manhole to fresh water tanks (port and starboard)
67. Watertight manhole to reserve feed water tanks (port and starboard)
68. Oiltight manhole to oil fuel tanks (filling) (port and starboard)
69. Oiltight manhole to oil fuel tanks (filling) (port)
70. Watertight manhole to save all
71. Drain (port and starboard)
72. Drain cock
73. Control rod
74. Bilge suction
75. Fresh water sounding (port and starboard)
76. Fresh water suction (port and starboard)
77. Reserve feed water sounding (port and starboard)
78. Reserve feed water suction (port and starboard)
79. Bilge suction
80. Oil fuel tank sounding (port and starboard)
81. Tank suction (port and starboard)
82. Bilge suction to magazine and save all
83. Oil bilge
84. Galley stove oil fuel suction
85. Oil fuel sucton (port and starboard)
86. Oil fuel tank sounding (port and starboard)
87. Bilge suction to forward boiler room (CL)
88. Oil fuel suction (port and starboard)
89. Oil fuel tank sounding (port and starboard)
90. Bilge suction to aft boiler room (port and starboard)
91. Forward engine room bilge suction
92. Aft engine room bilge suction
93. Drain (port and starboard)
94. Drain cock
95. Control rod
96. Drain
97. Drain (port and starboard)

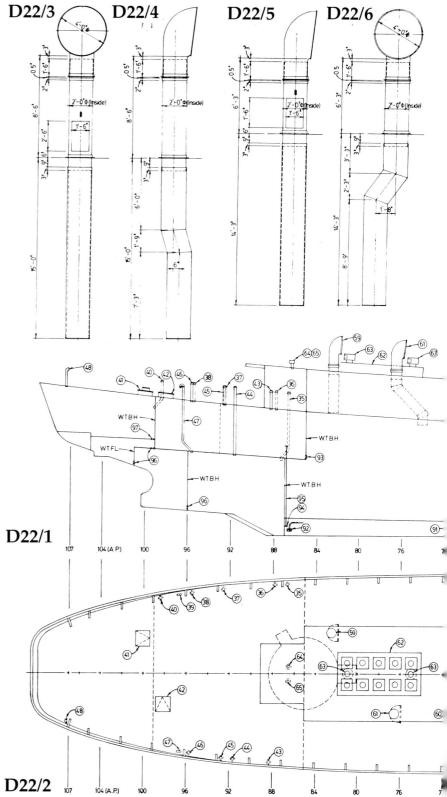

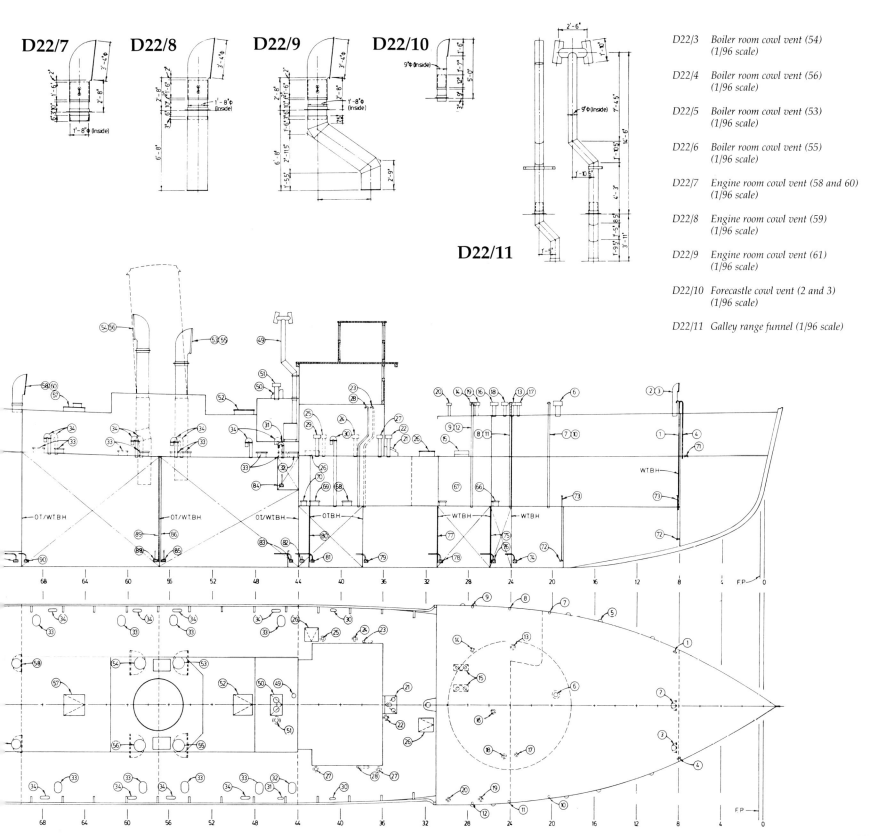

D22/3 Boiler room cowl vent (54) (1/96 scale)
D22/4 Boiler room cowl vent (56) (1/96 scale)
D22/5 Boiler room cowl vent (53) (1/96 scale)
D22/6 Boiler room cowl vent (55) (1/96 scale)
D22/7 Engine room cowl vent (58 and 60) (1/96 scale)
D22/8 Engine room cowl vent (59) (1/96 scale)
D22/9 Engine room cowl vent (61) (1/96 scale)
D22/10 Forecastle cowl vent (2 and 3) (1/96 scale)
D22/11 Galley range funnel (1/96 scale)

E Spars and rigging

E1 RIGGING PROFILE (1/384 scale)

Masts and yards
- A Fore mast (Douglas fir)
- B Fore yard (signal yard) (Douglas fir)
- C Main mast (Douglas fir)
- D Main yard (Douglas fir)
- E Main yard gaff
- F Jackstaff (hinged) (Douglas fir)
- G Ensign staff (portable – on starboard side) (Douglas fir)
- H Overtaking light staff (portable – on port side) (Douglas fir)

Rigging
1. Fore stay – 2in flexible steel wire rope
2. Triatic stay – 1¾in FSWR (galvanised)
3. Foremast shrouds (2 pairs) – 2in FSWR (galvanised)
4. Foremast backstays (2 pairs) – 2in FSWR (galvanised)
4a. Fore yard gantlines – 2¼in Manila
5. Fore yard standing lifts – 1¼in FSWR
6. Fore yard braces – ¾in FSWR
7. Mainmast shrouds (2 pairs) – 2in FSWR (galvanised)
7b. Main yard gantlines – 2¼in Manila
8. Main yard standing lifts – 1¼in FSWR
9. Main yard braces – ¾in FSWR
10. Mainmast gaff standing lift – 1in FSWR
11. Vangs (1 pair) – ¾in FSWR
12. Funnel guys (4 in no) – 1½in FSWR
13. Davit guys and span – 1½in FSWR
14. Boat falls – 2½in Manila
15. Life lines – 2½in Manila
16. Jacob's ladder to fore and main masts (not shown) – sides 1¼in FSWR set up with 1½in Manila lashings at deck. Hardwood rungs inserted into side wires and seized in place. Ladder braced to mast
17. Whistle pull – ¾in copper wire
18. Siren pull – ¾in copper wire
19. Signal halyards (4 pairs) – 1⅛in white hemp
20. Signal halyards – alternative location
21. Halyards (2 pairs) – 1½in white hemp
22. Jackstaff flag halyards (2 pairs) – ¾in white hemp
23. Ensign staff halyards (2 pairs) – ¾in white hemp
24. Tricing line and downhauler – 1¼in Manila (with 4in wood block)
25. Jackstays (2 in no, for lamp cage) – ¾in FSWR; lamp cage tricing line and downhauler – 1¼in Manila
26. Jackstays (2 in no, for lamp cage) – ¾in FSWR; lamp cage tricing line and downhauler – 1¼in Manila

Aerials
27. Low frequency transmitting aerials (4 in no)
28. Low frequency lead
29. High frequency transmitting aerial
30. High frequency lead
31. Transmitting aerial halyards – ¾in FSWR secured to 1½in Manila tail lines by shackles
32. DF sense aerial

Miscellaneous rigging items (not shown)
33. AS davit (port and starboard on forecastle)
    - guys – 1½in FSWR with 1½in Manila lashings
    - dome inhauler wire
    - tackle in AS comp – two 6in blocks, falls 1½in hemp
34. Ammunition davit (4in gun)
    - 6in gin block
    - 2½in white hemp runners
35. Davit for officers' store
36. Ammunition davit (2pdr gun)
37. Depth charge davits (4 in no)
    - two 6in wood blocks, IIB
    - falls, 2½in white hemp
38. Minesweeping gallows
39. Training davits (2 in no)
40. 10cwt derrick
    - guys
    - blocks
    - falls
41. Sounding boom
    - guys
    - lift
    - outhauler

Lights
1. Anchor light
2. Steaming light – electric
3. Steaming light – oil
4. Steaming light – electric
5. Steaming light – oil
6. Side light (port and starboard)
7. Overtaking light
8. Overtaking light on portable staff (not shown)

E4

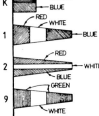

E5

E2 MAINMAST
E2/1 *Mainmast (1/96 scale)*
E2/2 *Mainmast step (no scale)*
E2/3 *Spider band (no scale)*
E2/4 *Band for gooseneck (no scale)*
E2/5 *Band for gaff standing lift (no scale)*
E2/6 *Hounds (no scale)*
E2/7 *Mast top (no scale)*

E3 FOREMAST
E3/1 *Foremast (1/96 scale)*
E3/2 *Foremast step (no scale)*
E3/3 *Partners (no scale)*
E3/4 *Crow's nest support (no scale)*
E3/5 *Upper hounds (no scale)*
E3/6 *Mast top (no scale)*

E4 RIGGING SCREW (1/32 scale)

E5 FLEXIBLE STEEL WIRE ROPE CONNECTOR (1/8 scale)

E6 INSULATOR (1/32 scale)
Lightweight break up insulator for LF transmitting aerial

E7 PENNANT NUMBER (no scale)

E7

E6

E1

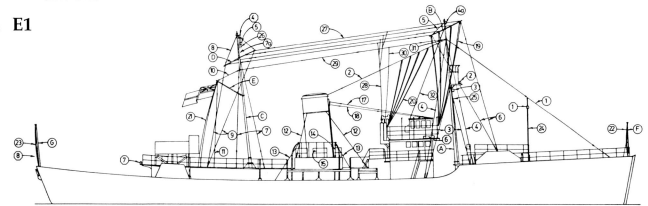

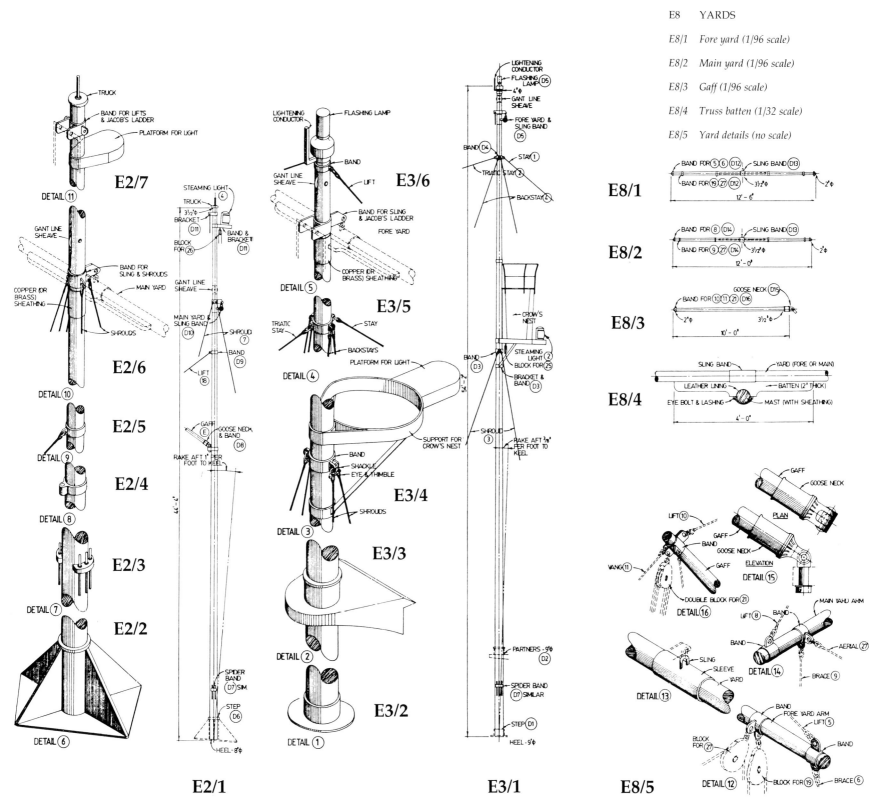

F Fittings

F1 **CARLEY FLOAT** (1/48 scale)
Pattern No 20, 5ft × 10ft, capacity 20

F1/1 Elevation
F1/2 Plan

F2 **BOLLARD** (1/32 scale)

F2/1 End elevation
F2/2 Side elevation
F2/3 Plan
F2/4 Isometric view (no scale)

F3 **FAIRLEAD** (1/32 scale)

F3/1 End elevation
F3/2 Side elevation
F3/3 Plan
F3/4 Isometric view (no scale)

F4 **KELVIN MARK IV SOUNDING MACHINE** (1/32 scale)

F4/1 End elevation
F4/2 Side elevation
F4/3 Plan
F4/4 Isometric view (no scale)

F5 **CARRIER AND BLOCK** (1/16 scale)

F5/1 End elevation
F5/2 Side elevation

F6 **SOUNDING AND 10cwt DERRICK BOOM (INTERCHANGEABLE)**

F6/1 Boom (1/96 scale)

F6/2 Sounding boom gooseneck, elevation and plan (1/16 scale)

1 Sounding boom
2 Gooseneck
3 Bulwark

F6/3 Boom end (no scale)

1 Boom
2 Band
3 Guy
4 Topping lift
5 Outhauler

F6/4 10cwt derrick gooseneck, elevation and plan (1/16 scale)

1 Boom
2 Gooseneck
3 Bracket on casing

F6/5 10cwt derrick end (no scale)

1 Boom
2 Band
3 Lifting tackle
4 Topping lift tackle
5 Guy

F7 **ROPE REEL** (1/32 scale)

F7/1 End elevation
F7/2 Side elevation
F7/3 Plan
F7/4 Isometric view (no scale)

1 Barrel
2 A frame
3 Top cross bar
4 Crank handle (removable)
5 Pulley belt
6 Brake
7 Brake handle
8 Pin and keeper chain

F8 **VOICE PIPE** (1/8 scale)

F8/1 End elevation
F8/2 Side elevation
F8/3 Plan

1 Pipe (copper tubing)
2 Brass nut
3 Hinge
4 Copper cone
5 Name plate
6 Copper lid
7 Mouthpiece
8 Knob

F8/4 Voice pipe stand elevation (1/32 scale)

1 Copper cone
2 Nut
3 Support bracket
4 Pipe (copper tubing)
5 Flange

126

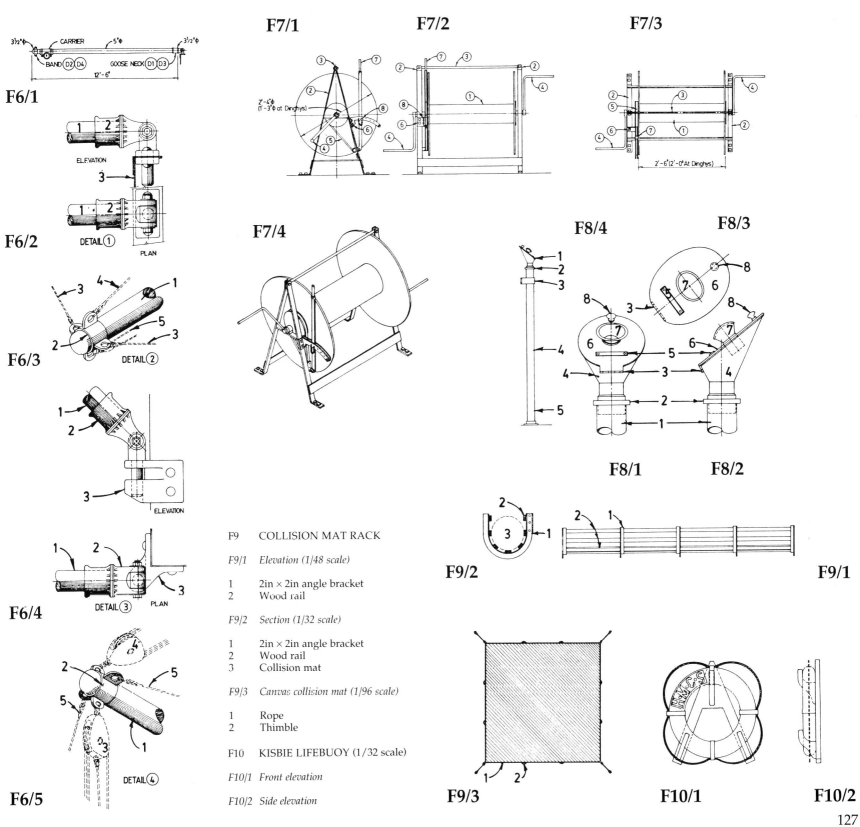

F Fittings

F11 FIRE BUCKET RACK (1/32 scale)

F11/1 Section

F11/2 Side elevation

F11/3 Plan

F11/4 Isometric view (no scale)

1 Teak rack
2 Bucket

F12 LIFE BELT RACK (1/32 scale)

F12/1 Section

F12/2 Side elevation

F12/3 Plan

F12/4 Isometric view (no scale)

1 Teak rack
2 Canvas cover

F13 DARKENING SHIP SCREENING LOCKER (TEAK) (1/32 scale)

F13/1 Front elevation

F13/2 Side elevation

F13/3 Plan

F13/4 Isometric view (no scale)

1 Hinge
2 Hasp

F14 LOCK BOX FOR MAGAZINE FLOODING VALVES (STEEL) (1/32 scale)

F14/1 Front elevation

F14/2 Side elevation

F14/3 Plan

F14/4 Isometric view (no scale)

1 Hinge
2 Lug and fly nut
3 Hasp

F15 WASH DECK LOCKER (1/32 scale)

F15/1 Front elevation

F15/2 Side elevation

F15/3 Plan

F15/4 Isometric view (no scale)

1 Hinge
2 Hasp

F16 BOXES ON COMPASS PLATFORM (1/32 scale)

Four in all for Not Under Command balls, recognition lights and steam signal cones

F16/1 Front elevation

F16/2 Side elevation

F16/3 Plan

F16/4 Isometric view (no scale)

1 Hinge
2 Hasp
3 Pipe rail
4 Metal support pan
5 Bracket

F17 FLAG LOCKER (1/32 scale)

F17/1 Section

F17/2 Elevation

F17/3 Isometric view (no scale)

1 Teak flag locker
2 Canvas shroud

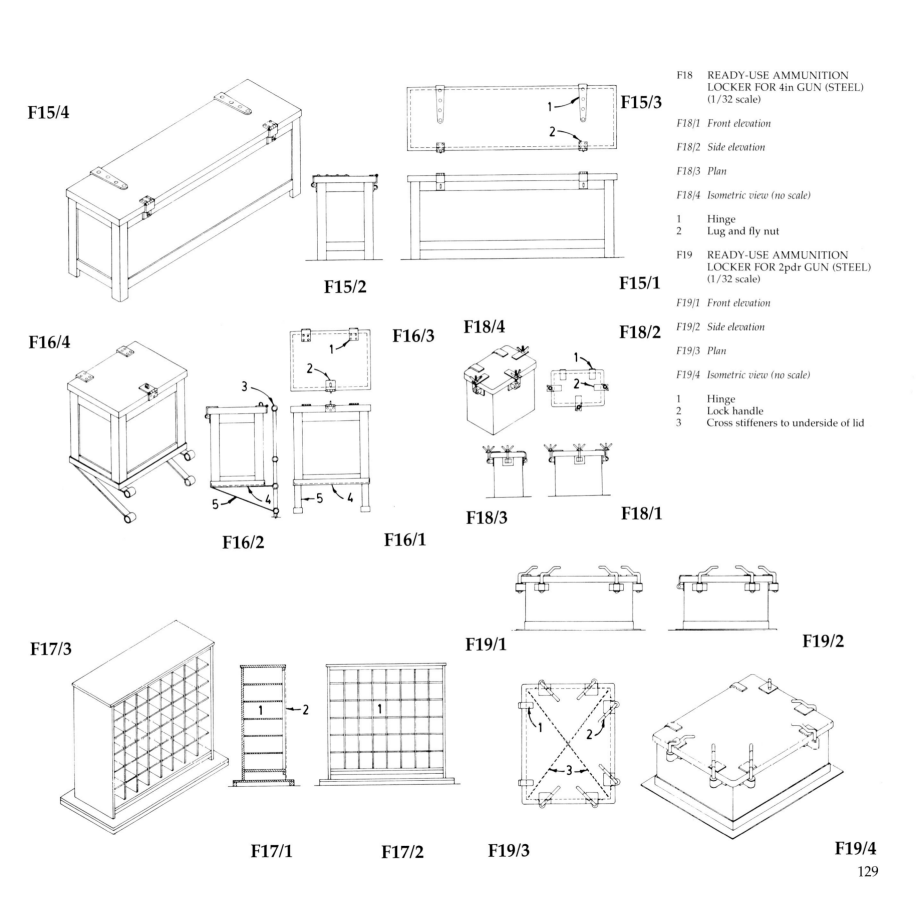

F Fittings

F20 VEGETABLE BIN AND BEEF SCREEN (1/32 scale)

F20/1 *Front elevation*

F20/2 *Side elevation*

F20/3 *Plan*

F20/4 *Isometric view (no scale)*

1 Teak vegetable bin
2 Teak beef screen
3 Hinge
4 Hasp
5 Mushroom vent
6 Vent holes
7 Copper screening

F21 5in DOWNTON HAND PUMP (1/32 scale)

F21/1 *Front elevation*

F21/2 *Side elevation*

F21/3 *Plan*

F21/4 *Isometric view (no scale)*

F22 FIREWORKS TANK (STEEL) (1/32 scale)

F22/1 *Front elevation*

F22/2 *Side elevation*

F22/3 *Plan*

F22/4 *Isometric view (no scale)*

1 Hinge
2 Lug and fly nut
3 Cross stiffeners to underside of lid

F23 WHISTLE (1/16 scale)

F23/1 *Front elevation*

F23/2 *Side elevation*

F23/3 *Isometric view (no scale)*

F24 SIREN (1/16 scale)

F24/1 *Front elevation*

F24/2 *Side elevation*

F24/3 *Isometric view (no scale)*

F25 10in SIGNALLING LAMP (1/32 scale)

F25/1 *Front elevation*

F25/2 *Rear elevation*

F25/3 *Side elevation*

F25/4 *Side elevation*

F25/5 *Plan*

F25/6 *Isometric view (no scale)*

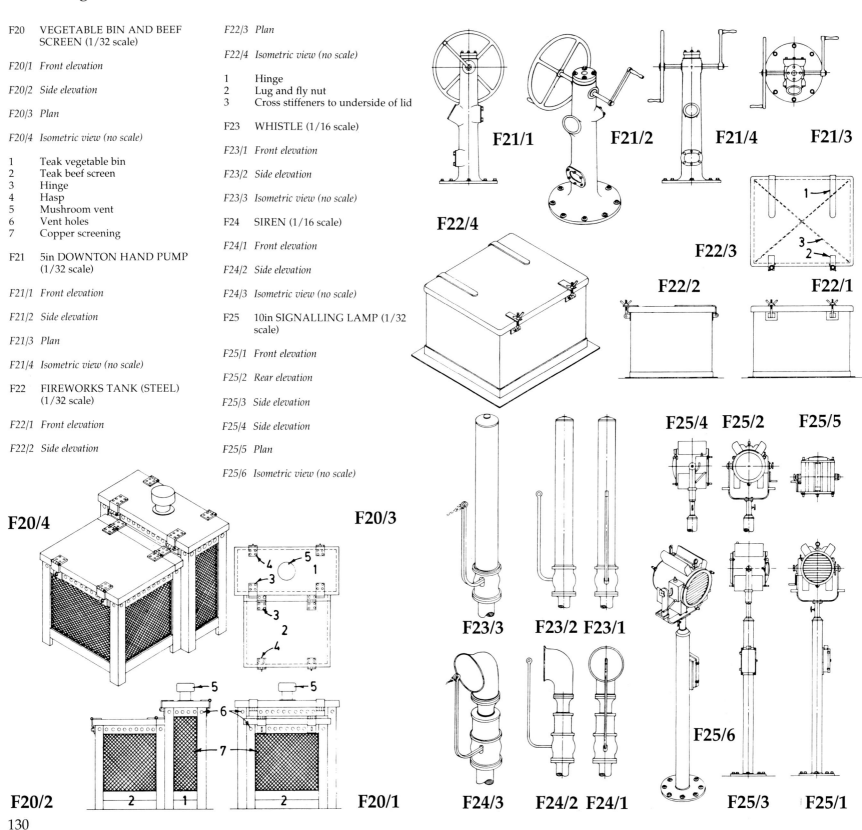

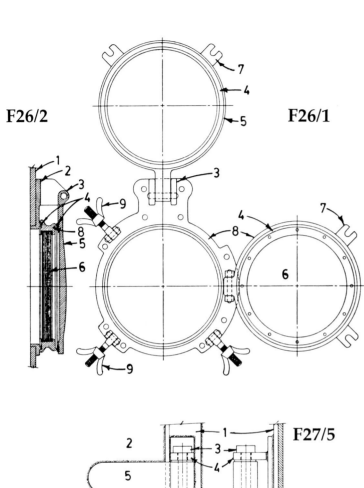

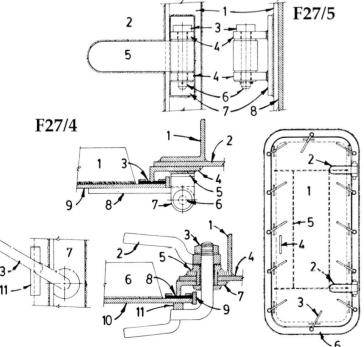

F26 SCUTTLE (1/8 scale)

All scuttles are hinged on the fore side.

F26/1 Elevation

F26/2 Section

1. Shell
2. Brass frame
3. Brass hinge
4. India rubber
5. Cast iron deadlight
6. Illuminator
7. Lug
8. Brass frame
9. Brass butterfly nut and screw

F27 WATERTIGHT DOORS

F27/1 Elevation (1/32 scale)

1. Door
2. Hinge
3. Clip and wedge
4. Handle
5. 3in × ½in stiffeners welded to reverse side
6. ⅜in door frame (welded)

F27/2 Frame and clip section (1/8 scale)

1. 3½in × 3½in × .34 oa stiffener
2. Handle
3. Nut
4. Bulkhead
5. Boss, bush and washers
6. 3in × ½in stiffener
7. Door frame
8. India rubber
9. 1in × ⅜in brass
10. Door
11. Wedge

F27/3 Clip elevation (1/8 scale)

F27/4 Hinge section (1/8 scale)

1. Stiffener
2. Bulkhead
3. India rubber
4. Door frame
5. Hinge plate
6. Pin
7. Lug
8. Hinge strap
9. Door

F27/5 Hinge elevations (1/8 scale)

1. Door frame
2. Door
3. Pin head
4. Lug
5. Hinge strap
6. Pin and cotter

7. Hinge plate
8. Bulkhead

F28 NON-WATERTIGHT DOOR

F28/1 Elevation (1/32 scale)

1. Door
2. 1in × 1in × ⅛in angle door stiffeners
3. Bulkhead stiffeners
4. Hinge
5. Lockset
6. Cabin hook and eye
7. Keeper (1½in × 1½in × ⅛in angle, 4in long)

F28/2 Hinge section and elevation (1/8 scale)

1. Bulkhead
2. Door
3. 1in × 1in × ⅛in angle door stiffener
4. Bulkhead stiffener
6. Brass pin (riveted over)

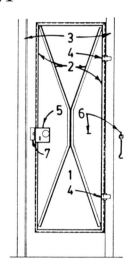

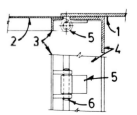

F Fittings

F29 WATERTIGHT HATCH, PLAN (1/32 scale)

1 Hinge
2 Lug and fly nut
3 Cross stiffeners to underside of lid

F30 OILTIGHT MANHOLE, PLAN (1/32 scale)

1 Hinge
2 Lug and fly nut

F31 HATCH COAMING (1/8 scale)

F31/1 Section

1 Deck plating
2 3in × 3in × .34 oa coaming bar
3 Coaming
4 Hinge plate
5 Clip plate
6 ½in diameter pin
7 Hinge
8 India rubber
9 Cross stiffeners
10 Butterfly nut and screw
11 Clip (lug)
12 Hatch cover

F31/2 Clip plan

1 Butterfly nut and screw
2 2in × ¼in clip

F32 GALLEY SKYLIGHT (1/8 scale)
Deadlight is not shown.

F32/1 Section

F32/2 Steel illuminator cover plan

F32/3 Hinge plan

1 Hinge
2 Steel ring
3 ⅝in glass illuminator (set in red lead putty)
4 Skylight cover
5 Lug with steel pin
6 Brass pin and keeper chain
7 1¾in × 5⁄16in opener
8 3in × 3in × .34 oa coaming bar
9 Deck plating
10 2in × 5⁄16in lug with ⅜in filler
11 Skylight coaming
12 Weld

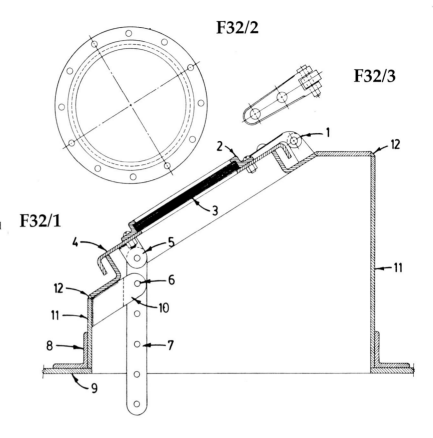

F32/2

F32/3

F32/1

F29

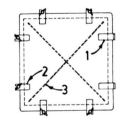

F30

F33 ENGINE ROOM SKYLIGHT (1/16 scale)

F33/1 Section

F33/2 Plan

1 Butterfly nut and clip
2 Hinge
3 Hinged deadlight
4 Handle
5 Steel ring
6 Skylight cover
7 3in × 3in × .34 oa coaming bar
8 India rubber
9 ¾in glass illuminator (set in red lead putty)
10 Lugs
11 Brass pin and keeper chain
12 Opener
13 3in × 3in × .34 oa stiffener
14 Deck plating

F34 PORTABLE JACKSTAFF (1/48 scale)

F34/1 End elevation

F34/2 Side elevation

F34/3 Plan

1 Truck
2 1¼in diameter pipe staff
3 Jackstaff (1¾in pipe)
4 Halyard cleat (¾in white hemp)
5 Bracket/clamp
6 Pipe brace
7 Bracket
8 Pipe rail socket
9 Brace foot

F34/4 Bracket detail (no scale)

1 1¼in diameter pipe staff
2 Bracket

F34/5 Truck detail (no scale)

1 Truck
2 1¼in diameter pipe staff
3 Halyard sheaves

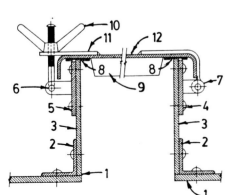

F31/1

F31/2

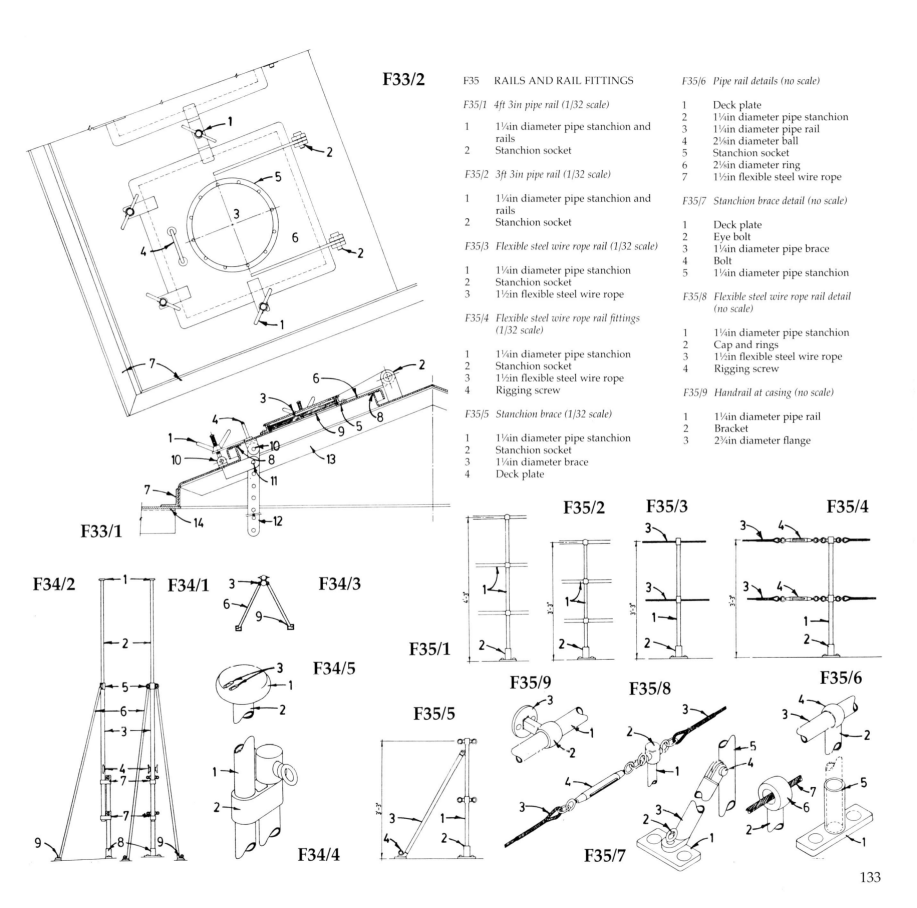

F Fittings

F36 ANCHOR WINDLASS (1/48 scale)

F36/1 Starboard elevation

F36/2 Plan

F36/3 Forward elevation

F36/4 Aft elevation

1. Anchor
2. Hawse pipe
3. Ring
4. Teak bed
5. Steel plate
6. Cast hawse rubber
7. 1$\frac{7}{16}$in stud link anchor cable
8. Blake screw stopper
9. Bottle screw
10. Deck ring
11. Windlass bedplate
12. Crank disk
13. Piston rod
14. Driving gear
15. Frame
16. Warping drum
17. Shaft
18. Cylinder
19. Gypsy
20. Clutch
21. Band brake
22. Brake control handle
23. Multiplying lever
24. Clutch control handle
25. 2in steam supply and valve
26. 2½in steam exhaust and valve
27. Chain pipe
28. Gear
29. Voice pipe
30. Reversing valve

F37 BOWER ANCHOR (1/48 scale)
Two carried, 22cwt (2464lb); 165 fathoms (990ft)
1$\frac{7}{16}$in stud link chain cable; hawsers and warps
100 fathoms 3½in FSWR.

1. Shank
2. Ring
3. Crown
4. Arm
5. Fluke
6. Bill (pea)
7. Gravity bands
8. Tripping palm

F38 KEDGE ANCHOR (1/48 scale)
One carried.

1. Shank
2. Ring
3. Stock
4. Crown
5. Arms
6. Flukes
7. Bill (pea)
8. Gravity band

G Armament

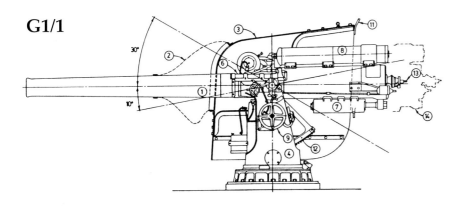

G1/1

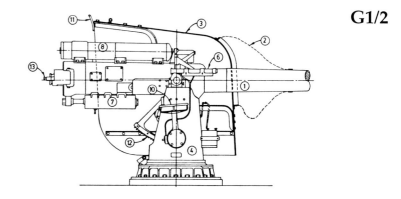

G1/2

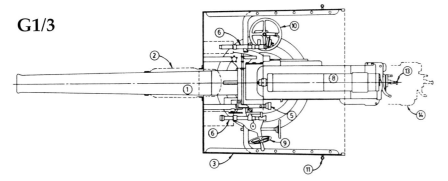

G1/3

G1	4in BREECH LOADING MARK IX GUN (1/48 scale)	
Muzzle velocity		2625ft/sec
Range		12,000 yards approx (6.8 miles)
Maximum elevation		30 degrees
Maximum depression		10 degrees

G1/1 Left elevation (layer's side)

G1/2 Right elevation (trainer's side)

G1/3 Plan

G1/4 Front elevation

G1/5 Gun shield elevation

G1/6 Gun shield plan

G1/7 Isometric view (no scale)

1. Gun barrel
2. Blast bag (canvas)
3. Gun shield
4. CPI mount
5. Open sight
6. Telescopic sight
7. Recoil and runout cylinder
8. Spring case
9. Elevating handwheel
10. Training handwheel
11. Rails
12. Elevating arc
13. Percussion striker
14. Recoil (18in maximum)

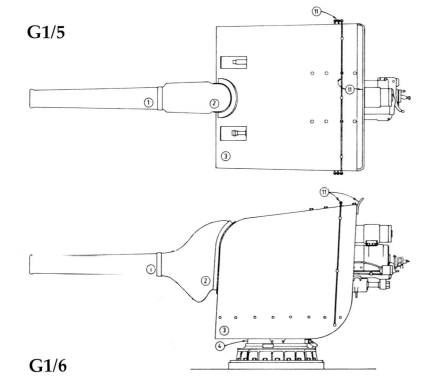

G1/5

G1/6

G1/4

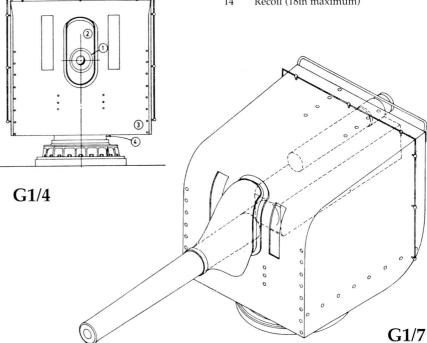

G1/7

G Armament

G2   4in SHELL HOLDER (1/16 scale)

G2/1   Front elevation

G2/2   Side elevation

G2/3   Rear elevation

G2/4   Plan

G2/5   Isometric view (no scale)

G3   HINGED STANCHION AT 4in GUN PLATFORM (1/32 scale)

G3/1   End elevation

G3/2   Side elevation

1   Gun platform
2   Stanchion
3   Hinge
4   Hinge portion of stanchion
5   Flexible steel wire rope

G4   AMMUNITION DAVIT AND GIN BLOCK (1/16 scale)

G4/1   End elevation

G4/2   Side elevation

1   Davit head
2   Shackle
3   Gin block

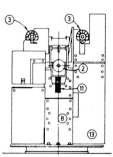
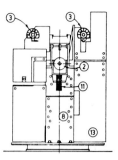

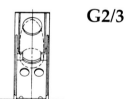

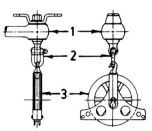

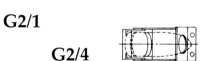
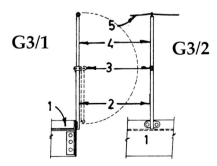
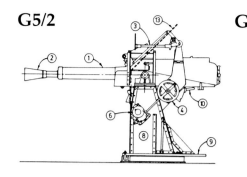
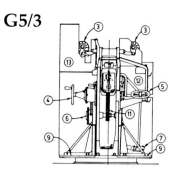
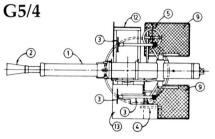
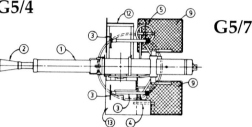
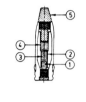
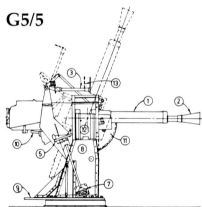

G5   2pdr QF MARK VIII GUN (1/48 scale)

G5/1   Front elevation

G5/2   Left elevation (layer's side)

G5/3   Rear elevation

G5/4   Plan

G5/5   Right elevation (trainer's side)

G5/6   Isometric view (no scale)

1   Gun barrel
2   Flame guard
3   Sight
4   Elevating handwheel
5   Training handwheel
6   Elevating gearbox
7   Training gearbox
8   Single Mark VIII mount
9   Racer plate
10   Firing handle
11   Elevating arc
12   Ammunition box
13   Shield

G5/7   2pdr HE/HV shell (1/8 scale)

1   Igniter
2   Paper tube
3   Powder pellet
4   Exploder
5   Percussion fuse

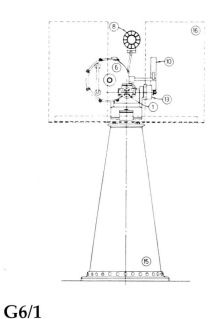

G6/1

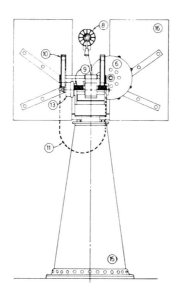

G6/2

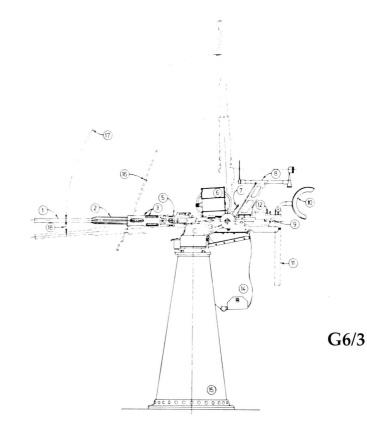

G6/3

G6 20mm OERLIKON MACHINE GUN (1/32 scale)

G6/1 Front elevation

G6/2 Rear elevation

G6/3 Side elevation

G6/4 Plan

1 Gun barrel
2 Cooling vanes (omitted from later guns)
3 Barrel spring casing and springs
4 Double loading stop
5 Buffer
6 Magazine
7 Magazine catch lever
8 Sight (200 knot)
9 Hand grip
10 Shoulder rest
11 Harness (leather)
12 Trigger
13 Trunnion and compensating spring
14 Cartridge case collecting bag (canvas)
15 Pedestal
16 Shield
17 57 degree maximum elevation
18 5 degree maximum depression

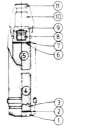 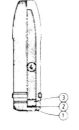

G6/5   **G6/6**

G6/5 Section of high explosive shell with tracer (no scale)

G6/6 Section of projectile tracer (no scale)

1 Base plug
2 Closing disc
3 Priming composition
4 Tracer composition
5 HE filling
6 Paper disc
7 Boxcloth washer
8 Detonator
9 Rear disc
10 Percussion fuse
11 Closing disc

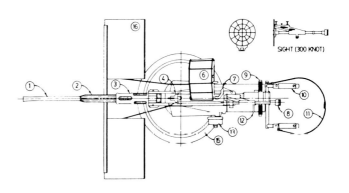

G6/4

G Armament

G7 DEPTH CHARGE THROWER (1/48 scale)

G7/1 Front elevation
G7/2 Rear elevation
G7/3 Section
G7/4 Side elevation
G7/5 Plan
G7/6 Plan of base

1 Depth charge
2 DC carrier tray
3 Wire strop
4 Barrel
5 Expansion chamber
6 Carrier piston
7 Firing gear
8 Base plate
9 Hold down strop
10 Ring

G8 MARK IV DEPTH CHARGE THROWER (1/48 scale)

G8/1 Front elevation
G8/2 Rear elevation
G8/3 Section
G8/4 Side elevation
G8/5 Plan
G8/6 Plan of base

1 Depth charge
2 DC carrier tray
3 Wire strop
4 Barrel
5 Expansion chamber
6 Arrester cylinder pipe
7 Arrester cylinder
8 Strop shipping and gear
9 Exhaust port
10 Carrier piston
11 Surge tank
12 Firing gear
13 Base plate

G9 DEPTH CHARGE CHUTE (1/48 scale)

G9/1 Forward elevation (port side)
G9/2 Side elevation (port side, from inboard)
G9/3 Plan of bottom rails (port side)
G9/4 Plan of top rails (port side)
G9/5 Smoke candle elevation (1/32 scale)
G9/6 Smoke candle plan (1/32 scale)

1 Bottom rails
2 Depth charge
3 Top rails
4 Stanchion
5 Release lever
6 Release mechanism
7 Opening in bulwark
8 Smoke candle
9 Smoke candle rack
10 Bulwark
11 Brace

G9/1

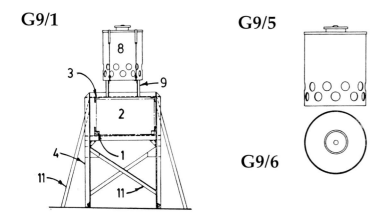

G9/5

G9/6

G9/2

G9/3

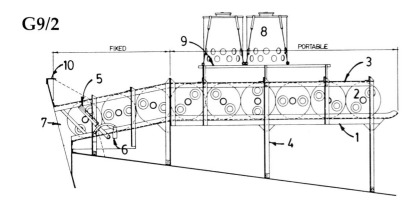

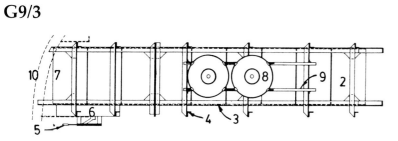

G9/4

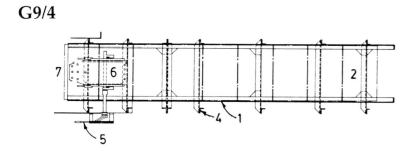

G10   MARK VII DEPTH CHARGE
      (1/16 scale)

G10/1 *Top elevation*

G10/2 *Bottom elevation*

G10/3 *Section*

1   Ballast weight
2   Steel case
3   Explosive filling
4   Primer placer
5   Primer
6   Centre tube
7   Pistol
8   Protective rubber cover
9   Detonator
10 Primer charge
11 Filling hole and bung
12 Depth setting key
13 Lifting ring

G11   DEPTH CHARGE STOWAGE
      (1/48 scale)

G11/1 *End elevation*

G11/2 *Side elevation*

G11/3 *Plan*

G11/4 *Isometric view of chocks (no scale)*

1   Carrier piston
2   Depth charge
3   DC carrier tray
4   Wire strop
5   Stowage lashing
6   Lashing ring
7   Stowage bracket
8   Wood chock
9   3in × 3in angle and steel chock

G10/2   **G10/3**   **G10/1**

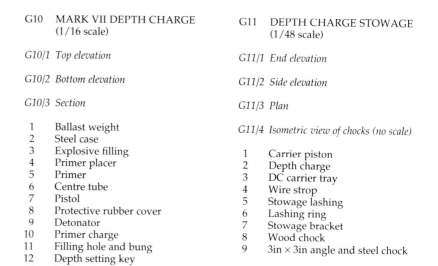

G11/1   **G11/2**   **G11/4**

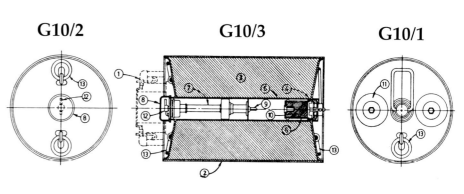

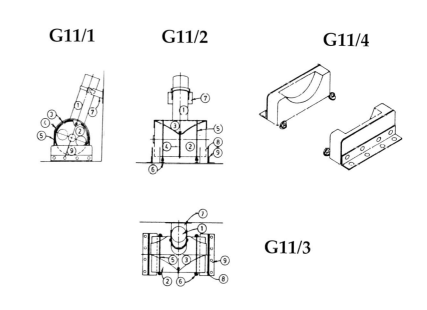

G11/3

G Armament

G12   HEDGEHOG (1/48 scale)

G12/1 *Aft elevation*
G12/2 *Starboard elevation*
G12/3 *Forward elevation*
G12/4 *Port elevation*
G12/5 *Longitudinal section*
G12/6 *Cross section*
G12/7 *Plan*

1   Base
2   Back shield
3   Shield brace
4   Spigot
5   Projectile
6   Handwheel (to control offset angle)
7   Ripple switch
8   Junction box
9   Safety switch
10 Stabiliser receiver
11 Control box
12 Arc of elevation display
13 Degree of offset display
14 Adjustable range input crank
15 Firing button
16 Lifting rings

G12/8   *Elevation of hedgehog projectile (1/16 scale)*
G12/9   *Plan (1/16 scale)*
G12/10 *Longitudinal section (1/16 scale)*
G12/11 *Section of projectile through drum and tail fin (1/16 scale)*

1   Spigot
2   Drum and tail fin
3   Tail tube
4   Cartridge firing contact
5   Cartridge
6   Projectile case
7   Explosive filling (32lb Torpex)
8   Primer
9   Fuse
10 Fuse cap
11 Clip

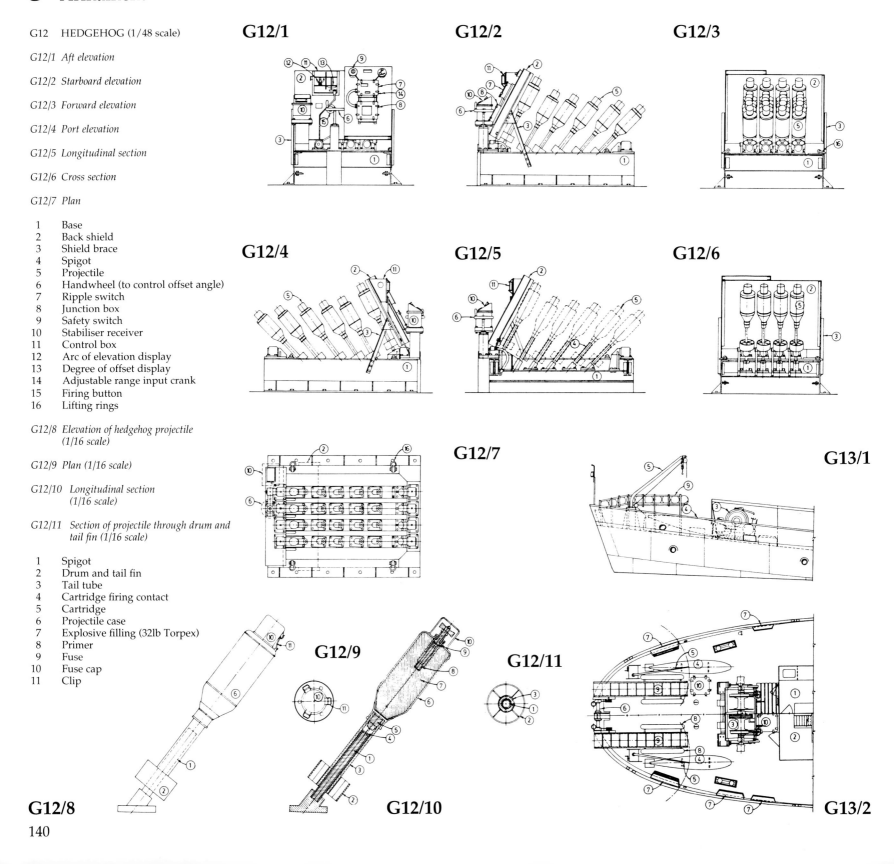

140

G14/1

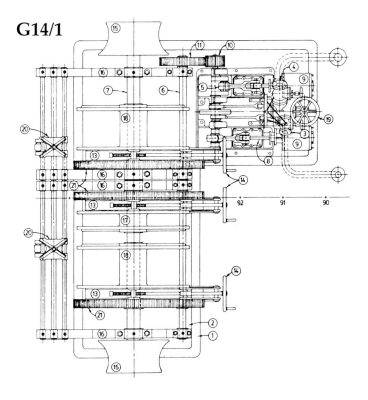

G13 MINESWEEPING ARRANGEMENTS (1/192 scale)

Arrangements shown are on a typical RN round stern vessel.

G13/1 Profile

G13/2 Plan

1. Galley
2. Passage
3. MS winch
4. MS float
5. Davit
6. MS fairleads
7. Kite/otter
8. Wood step
9. Depth charge rails
10. Hatch

G14 MINESWEEPING WINCH (1/48 scale)

G14/1 Plan

G14/2 Starboard elevation

G14/3 Port elevation

G14/4 Aft elevation

G14/5 Forward elevation

1. Teak bed
2. Winch bedplate
3. 2½in steam supply and valve
4. 3¼in steam exhaust and valve
5. Engine shaft (3½in diameter)
6. Second motion shaft (3½in diameter)
7. Third motion shaft (5½in diameter)
8. Piston rod
9. Cylinder (8in diameter, 9in stroke)
10. Driving gear
11. Second motion gear
12. Clutch
13. Band brake
14. Brake control wheel
15. Warping drum
16. Frame
17. Spool (kite wire)
18. Spool (float wire)
19. Stop valve and throttle
20. Spooling guide (jockey gear)
21. Spur wheel

G14/2

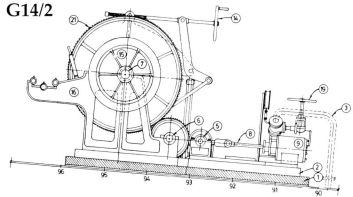

G14/3

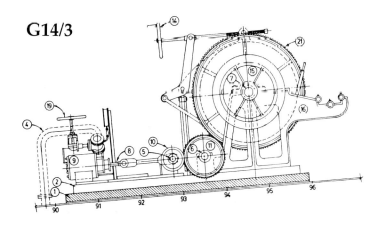

G14/4

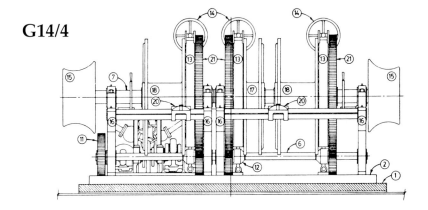

G14/5

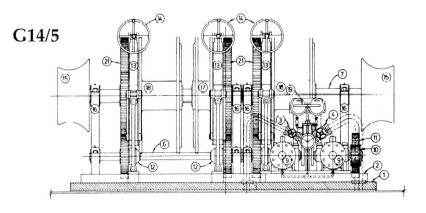

G Armament

G15 MINESWEEPING DAVIT
(1/48 scale)

G15/1 *End elvation*

G15/2 *Side elevation*

G15/3 *Plan*

1 Pedestal
2 Boom
3 Sheave
4 Lifting tackle for MS float
5 Lifting tackle for depth charges
6 Eyebolts
7 Lifting crank
8 Training crank

G16 MINESWEEPING FLOAT
(1/48 scale)

G16/1 *Aft elevation*

G16/2 *Side elevation*

G16/3 *Cross section*

G16/4 *Plan*

G16/5 *Isometric view of fin and stabiliser (no scale)*

G16/6 *Carrier rack (no scale)*

1 Minesweeping float
2 Marker pennant staff
3 Bracket
4 Lifting handle
5 Fin and stabiliser
6 Carrier rack
7 Bracket for MS wire
8 Weld

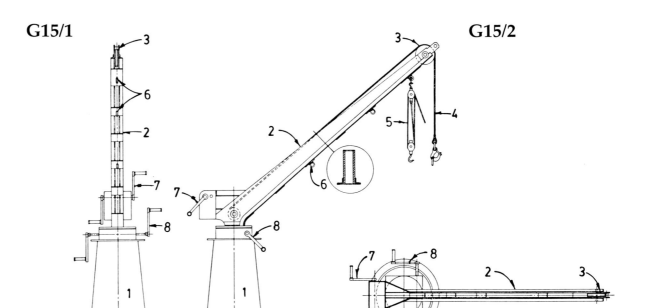

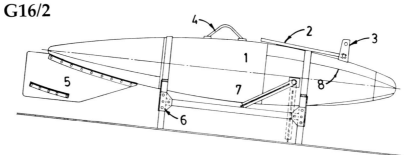

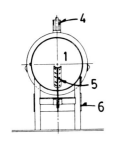

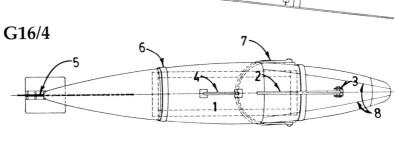

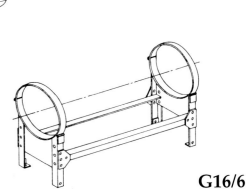

G17/1

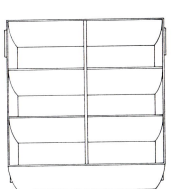

G17 MULTIPLANE KITE/OTTER (1/32 scale)

G17/1 Plan

G17/2 End elevation

G17/3 Side elevation

G17/4 Section

G17/5 Isometric view (no scale)

G18 HINGED GALLOWS FOR LIFTING DAN BUOYS (1/48 scale)

G18/1 End elevation

G18/2 Side elevation

G18/3 Plan

1. Gallows
2. Deck eye and pin
3. Bulwark
4. Lifting tackle
5. Shackle
6. Rings for lashing
7. Deck reinforce plate
8. Fairlead
9. Deck plating

G17/2 **G17/3** **G17/4** **G17/5**

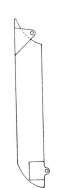  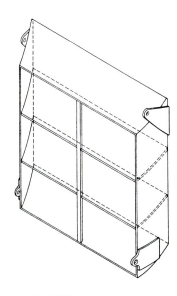

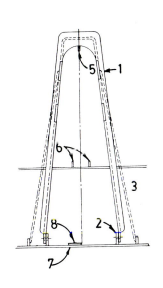 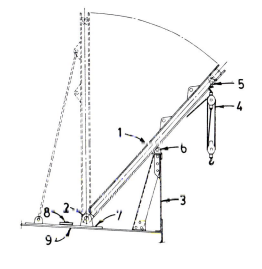 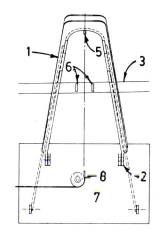

G18/1 **G18/2** **G18/3**

143

G Armament

G19 DAN BUOY DAVIT – PORTABLE
(1/48 scale)

G19/1 *End elevation*

G19/2 *Side elevation*

G19/3 *Plan*

1 Davit
2 Bracket
3 Brace
4 Deck plate and eyebolt
5 Pipe stanchion
6 Deck clip
7 Ring for lifting tackle

G19/4 *Isometric view of davit (no scale)*

1 Ring for lifting tackle
2 Davit
3 Bracket
4 Brace
5 Deck clip
6 Deck plate and eyebolt

G19/5 *Davit detail (no scale)*

1 Bolt
2 Deck clip
3 Pipe stanchion
4 Bracket
5 Davit

G19/6 *Dan buoy carrier/stanchion (no scale)*

G19/7 *Dan buoy (1/48 scale)*

G20 MAGNETIC MINESWEEPING
ARRANGEMENTS (1/192 scale)

G20/1 *Outboard profile*

G20/2 *Inboard profile*

G20/3 *Plan*

1 Line of casing (HMCS *Agassiz*)
2 Extended casing
3 LL MS reel
4 Roller fairlead
5 Davit
6 DC rails
7 Hatch
8 Grating
9 Smoke candles

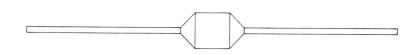

G19/7

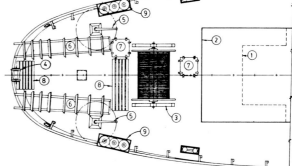

144

G21/1

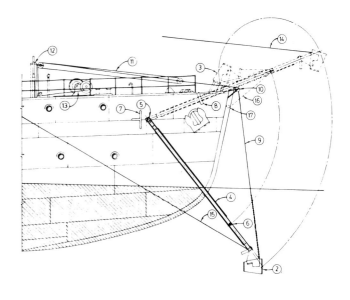

G21/2

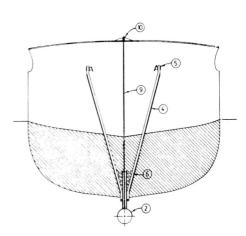

G21   ACOUSTIC MINESWEEPING
      ARRANGEMENTS (1/192 scale)

G21/1 Outboard profile

G21/2 Plan

G21/3 Bow elevation

G21/4 Details of acoustic hammer bucket (1/96 scale)

1 Acoustic hammer bucket
2 Acoustic hammer bucket (working position)
3 Acoustic hammer bucket (stowed position)
4 SA gear (A frame)
5 A frame pivot
6 Bucket pivot
7 Pivot guard
8 A frame stowage bracket
9 Inhauler
10 Inhauler roller fairlead
11 Inhauler tackle
12 Tackle stanchion
13 Anchor windlass
14 Topping lift
15 Backhauler
16 Bucket downhauler
17 Bucket downhauler sheave (port side)

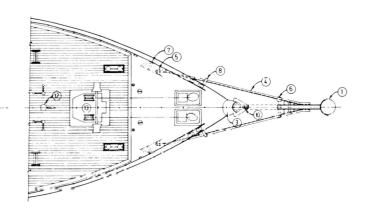

G21/3

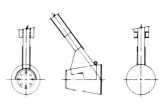

G21/4

H Ship's boat

H1   16ft DINGHY (1/48 scale)
16ft × 5ft, 9in × 2ft, 5in; capacity 16

H1/1   *Outboard profile*

H1/2   *Inboard profile*

H1/3   *Plan*

H1/4   *Section*

H1/5   *Stern elevation*

H1/6   *Bow elevation*

H1/7   *Sail plan (1/96 scale)*
Mast   12ft long from thwart, 3in diameter
Yard (sprit) 11ft 6in long, 1⅝in diameter
Oars   two 14ft long, two 10ft long

H1/8   *Isometric view (no scale)*

1. Stem
2. Sternpost
3. Stern knee
4. Keel
5. Hog
6. Keelson
7. Timbers (frames)
8. Plank
9. Top strake (gunwale)
10. Garboard strake
11. Stringer (shelf)
12. Capping
13. Thwart
14. Knee
15. Head sheets
16. Stern sheets
17. Ringbolt
18. Bottom boards
19. Socket for crutch
20. Sailing thwart (mast carling)
21. Knee
22. Mast
23. Mast step
24. Rudder
25. Pintle and gudgeon
26. Tiller
27. Transom
28. Transom knee

H2   PLAN OF BOAT PLATFORM
(1/96 scale)

1. Funnel top casing
2. 16ft dinghy
3. Boat platform
4. Pipe rail
5. Boat davit
6. Rope reel
7. Boat chock
8. Davit stay
9. Dinghy in lowering position

H1/1
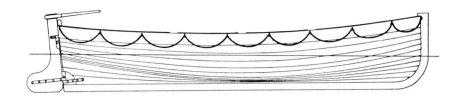

H1/6
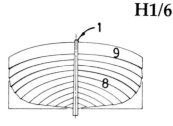

H1/2
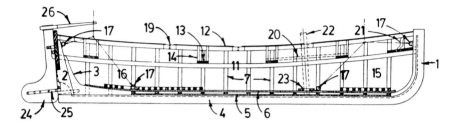

H1/4
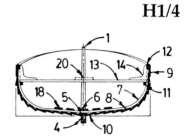

H1/3
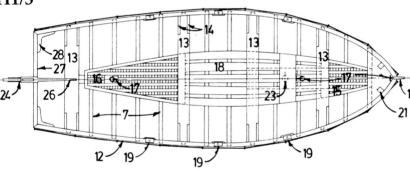

H1/5
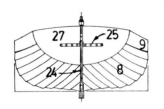

H1/8
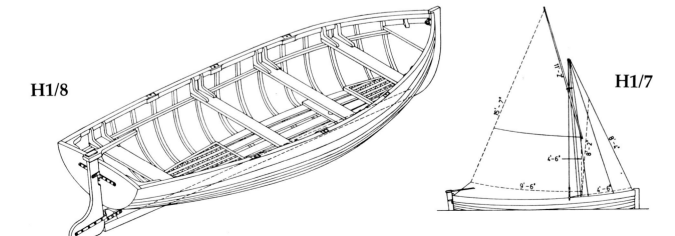

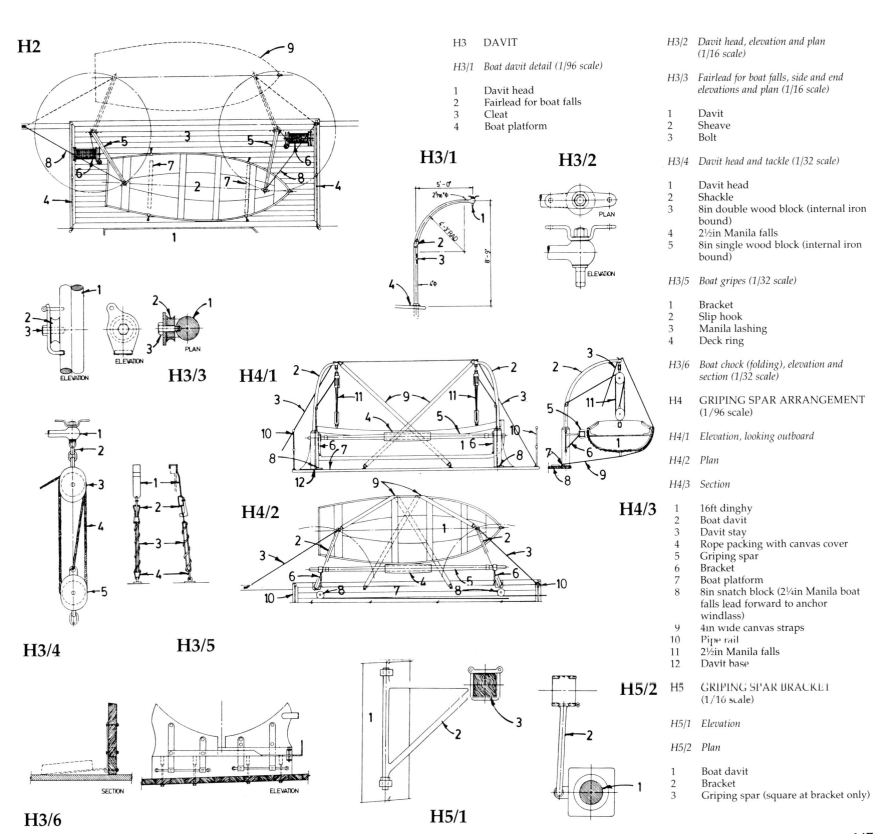

I Modified Flower and Castle class corvettes

I1 MODIFIED FLOWER CLASS CORVETTE HMCS *ATHOLL* (1/192 scale)

I1/1 Profile

1. Jackstaff
2. Fairlead
3. Main naval store
4. Fore peak
5. Chain pipes
6. Crew's mess space
7. Crew's accommodation
8. Chain locker
9. Store
10. Store
11. Asdic compartment
12. Ladder
13. Fresh water tanks
14. Instrument compartment
15. Provision and store rooms
16. Crew's accommodation
17. 4in magazine (starboard)
18. Lobby
19. Spirit room (port)
20. Crew's accommodation
21. Ship's office and canteen
22. Lobby
23. Codes office
24. Galley
25. Low power room
26. Gyro compass room
27. Officers' accommodation
28. Fuel oil tanks
29. 2pdr magazine
30. Air space
31. Boiler room
32. Reserve feed water
33. Engine room
34. Engineers' store
35. POs' accommodation
36. Aft peak tank
37. Steering compartment
38. Fairlead
39. Bollard
40. Anchor windlass
41. 4in QF Mark XIX gun
42. Splinter protection plate
43. Hedgehog
44. CO's office and cabin
45. 20-man Carley float
46. Wheel house
47. D/F loop
48. A/S hut
49. Wind deflector
50. Pelorus
51. Compass
52. 20mm Oerlikon
53. Anchor light
54. 10in signalling lamp
55. Aerial screen
56. Mast
57. Crow's nest
58. Yard
59. Type 291 radar antenna
60. 27ft whaler
61. Funnel casing
62. Funnel
63. Galley stove stack
64. ER vent
65. Supply vent to ER fan
66. Search light platform
67. 2pdr gun
68. 10-man Carley float
69. Depth charge thrower
70. Depth charge stowage
71. Smoke candles
72. DC stowage rails
73. DC rails
74. DC davit
75. Overtaking light

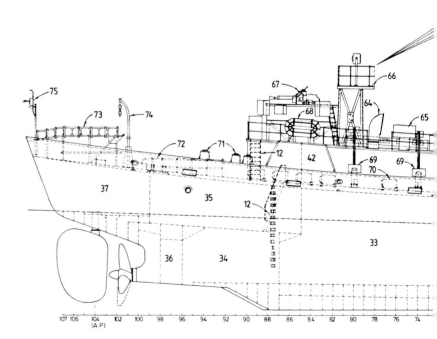

I1/1

148

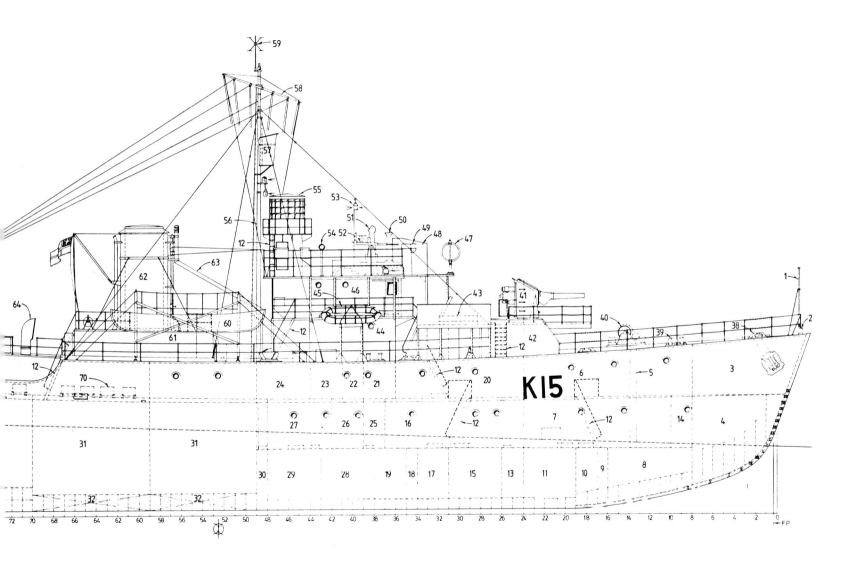

I Modified Flower and Castle class corvettes

I1/2 Plan of compass platform

1. A/S office
2. Chart recess
3. D/F loop
4. Pelorus
5. Compass
6. 18in high platform
7. 20mm Oerlikon
8. Very pistol
9. Wind deflector
10. Splinter matress
11. Oerlikon RU locker
12. Signalman's reading lamp
13. Oerlikon RU locker
14. Oerlikon RU locker
15. Locker for AM flags
16. Flag locker
17. Box for NUC balls
18. Box for NUC recognition lights
19. 10in signalling lamp
20. RDF office
21. Mast
22. Platform
23. Lantern
24. Opening

I1/3 Plan of gun platform and bridge deck

1. 4in QF Mark XIX gun
2. Hedgehog mounting
3. Ammunition hatch
4. Hedgehog RU locker
5. Helmet locker
6. 4in RU locker
7. 4in RU locker
8. Recess over companion
9. Hedgehog RU locker
10. 20-man Carley float
11. Hedgehog RU locker
12. Battery cupboard
13. Mast
14. Wheel house
15. W/T office
16. Chart room
17. Cupboard
18. Chart table
19. Chronometer box
20. Settee
21. Rocket flares
22. Table

I1/4 Plan of forecastle deck

1. Fairlead
2. Hawse pipes
3. Fairlead
4. Bollard
5. Anchor windlass
6. Reel
7. 4in gun mount
8. Rocket flares locker
9. Hedgehog support
10. Ammunition hatch
11. Companion
12. Chain
13. Bean bollard
14. SW2C office
15. CO's cabin
16. Lobby
17. Snowflake locker
18. Oerlikon magazine locker
19. Fireworks tank
20. Hatch
21. Galley stove stack
22. Mast
23. Galley skylight
24. Beef screen locker
25. 27ft whaler
26. 20-man Carley float
27. Sounding machine
28. Life raft
29. Fire buckets
30. Sounding boom
31. Vegetable locker
32. Compass
33. ER vent
34. Supply vent to ER fan
35. Potato locker
36. ER skylight
37. Searchlight platform
38. 2pdr gun platform
39. 10-man Carley float
40. Davit over DC thrower
41. Companion
42. 10cwt derrick
43. Ammunition locker
44. Wash deck locker

I1/5 Plan of upper deck

1. Main naval store
2. W/T hatch
3. Crew's mess space
4. Crew's accommodation
5. Crew's wash place
6. Lobby
7. Crew's WC
8. Canteen
9. Ship's office
10. Lobby
11. Codes office
12. Loan clothes store
13. Officers' WC
14. Officers' bath
15. Gunner's store
16. Store
17. Oiltight hatch
18. Passage
19. Sick cabin
20. Refrigerator
21. Provision issue room
22. Galley
23. Boiler room
24. FD fan room
25. Air lock
26. Engine room
27. DC stowage
28. DC thrower
29. Bollard
30. Securing straps for drums
31. POs' washplace
32. Shower
33. POs' WC
34. Smoke candles
35. 10cwt derrick
36. DC stowage rails
37. DC davit
38. DC rails
39. Roller fairlead
40. Hatch
41. Scuttle
42. 5in Downton pump

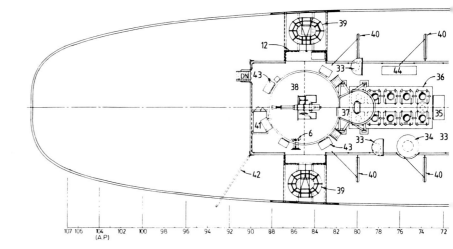

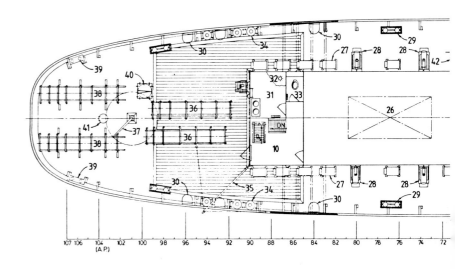

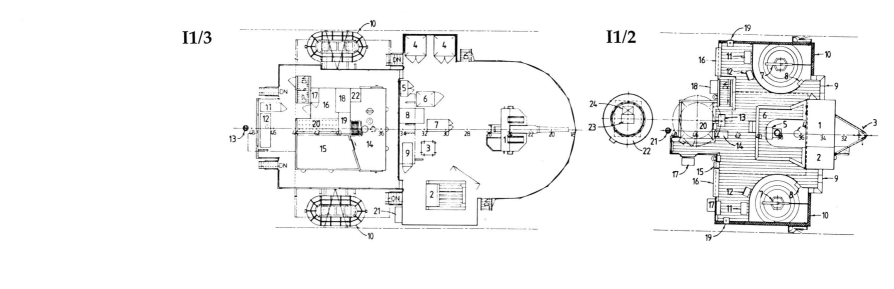

I1/3 **I1/2**

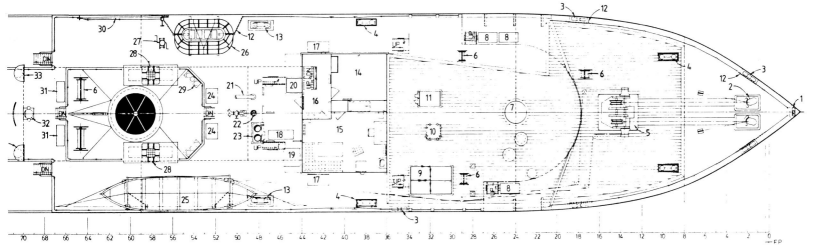

I1/4

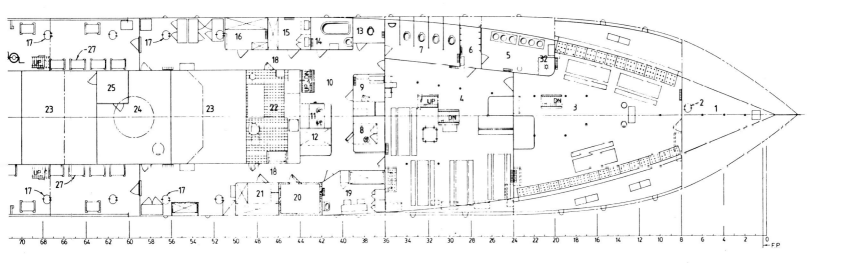

I1/5

151

I Modified Flower and Castle class corvettes

I1/6   Plan of lower deck

1   Fore peak
2   Instrument compartment
3   Crew's accommodation
4   Hatch
5   Hatch cover
6   Low power room
7   Gyro compass room
8   Lobby
9   Air space
10 Officer's cabin
11 Pantry
12 Ward room
13 OT/WT manhole
14 Boiler room
15 Oil fuel bunker
16 Engine room
17 Cabin/office
18 Cabin/office
19 POs' sleeping accommodation
20 POs' mess
21 Steering compartment

I1/7   Plan of hold

1   Fore peak
2   Chain locker
3   Naval store
4   Asdic compartment
5   Fresh water tank
6   Provision room
7   Store room
8   Spirit room
9   Lobby
10 4in magazine
11 4in shell room
12 Oil fuel bunker
13 2pdr magazine
14 Air space
15 Boiler room
16 Engine room
17 Engineers' store
18 Hatch cover
19 Aft peak tank

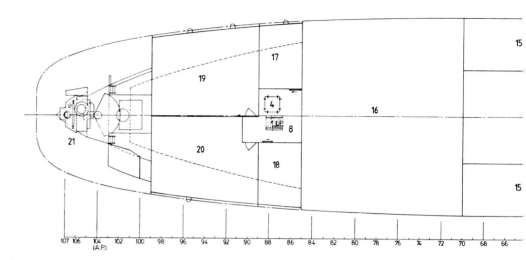

I1/6

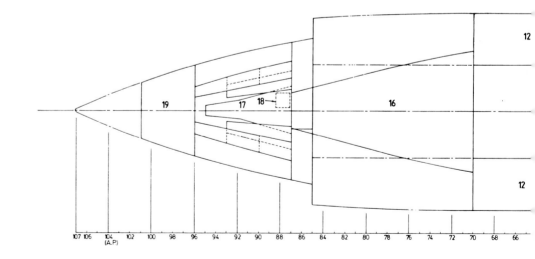

I1/7

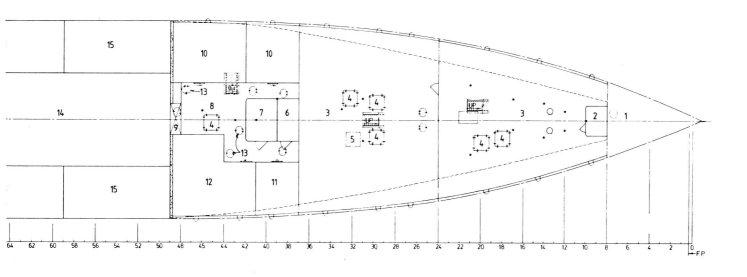
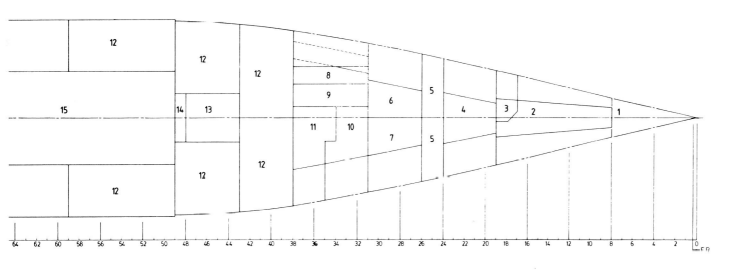

153

I Modified Flower and Castle class corvettes

I2   CASTLE CLASS CORVETTE
     HMCS *ARNPRIOR* (1/192 scale)

Length overall	252ft 0in
Length bp	225ft 0in
Breadth	36ft 8in
Depth (mean)	13ft 6in

I2/1   Profile

1. Paint and lamp room
2. Fore peak
3. Naval store
4. Chain locker
5. Cable locker
6. Store
7. Accommodation
8. Provision room and canteen store
9. A/S trunk
10. Pocket
11. A/S compartment
12. Type 1478
13. Fresh water tank
14. Seamen's mess
15. Accommodation
16. 4in magazine
17. Cold room/refrigeration machinery compartment
18. Lobby
19. Squid projectile room
20. Oerlikon magazine
21. Oil fuel
22. Low power room (port)
23. Offices, cabins and accommodation
24. Boiler room
25. Crew's heads and washplace
26. Engine room
27. Main feed water tank
28. Engineers' workshop
29. Lobby
30. Engineers' store and spirit room
31. Naval store and provision issue room
32. Gland compartment
33. Steering gear compartment
34. Jackstaff
35. Fairlead
36. Anchor windlass
37. 4in gun (Mark XIX)
38. 4in ready use locker
39. Shelter
40. Squid (DC mortar)
41. Squid handling room
42. Trunk
43. Accommodation
44. Derrick
45. Wheel house
46. Chart house
47. D/F outfit FM 12
48. Pelorus
49. Standard compass
50. Mark IIIA Oerlikon
51. 10in signalling lamp
52. 20in searchlight
53. Type 253 aerial
54. Outfit ASB Type 242
55. Type 25/M aerial
56. RDF Type 272
57. Outfit FM 4
58. W/T office
59. RDF house
60. BR vent
61. Aerials
62. Receiving aerials (port)
63. DF sense finder rec aerials
64. TBL aerials
65. Main aerials TBL
66. 27ft whaler
67. Funnel
68. Ensign gaff
69. FW tank
70. BR vent
71. Galley
72. Carley float
73. Coal bunker
74. Cowl vent
75. Gallows crane
76. Goal post mast
77. Mark IIIA Oerlikon
78. Spigot for loudhailer
79. ER skylight
80. Vegetable locker
81. Beef screen
82. Exhaust diesel
83. Floating off buoy
84. Potato locker
85. Inlet to diesel generator
86. Overtaking light
87. WT hatch
88. DC stowage
89. Davit
90. DC thrower
91. DC rails

I2/1

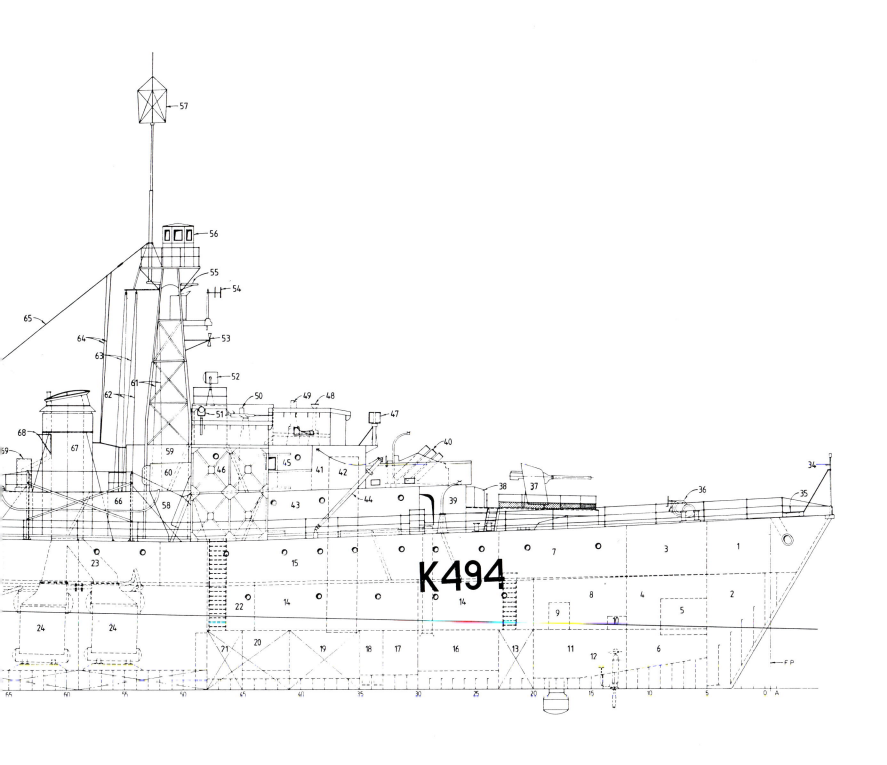

I Modified Flower and Castle class corvettes

I2/2   Plan of Oerlikon gun platform

1. Mark IIIA Oerlikon
2. Ready-use ammunition
3. Compass
4. Spigot for loudhailer

I2/3   Plan of top of galley

1. Carley float
2. Skylight
3. FW tank
4. ER vent

I2/4   Plan of bridge deck

1. Floatnet
2. Squid (DC mortar)
3. Trolley track
4. Davit
5. Squid handling room
6. Winch
7. Trunk
8. Wood flat
9. Wheel house
10. Signalman's desk
11. Binnacle
12. Wheel
13. ER telegraph
14. Signalman's confidential box
15. Chart house
16. Box for confidential books
17. Bed/settee
18. Ammunition trunk
19. Cresset flares
20. RDF house
21. BR vent

I2/5   Plan of compass platform

1. D/F outfit FM 12
2. Chart table
3. Pelorus
4. Standard compass
5. Aldis lamp
6. Step
7. Mark IIIA Oerlikon
8. Signal boxes
9. Ready-use ammunition
10. Wood platform
11. Flag locker
12. Snowflake locker
13. WT hatch (ammunition trunk)
14. Davit
15. A/S plot
16. Plot table
17. A/S office
18. Top of RDF house
19. Parachute and cable projector

I2/6   Plan of forecastle deck

1. Jackstaff
2. Fairlead
3. Chain pipe
4. Anchor windlass
5. Bollard
6. Reel
7. Gun platform
8. 4in gun (Mark XIX)
9. 4in RU locker
10. Rocket flare locker under
11. Breakwater
12. Rocket flare locker
13. A/S davit
14. Leadsman's platform
15. Shelter
16. Hoist
17. Ammunition trunk
18. Life saving net
19. Derrick (stowed)
20. Sounding machine
21. Sounding machine (stowed)
22. Skylight
23. Wash deck locker
24. Cabin
25. RPC compartment
26. Cabin
27. Lobby
28. WT trunk
29. Ship's office
30. CO's cabin
31. Cabin
32. Cabin
33. W/T office
34. Machinery compartment
35. Bean bollard
36. 16ft trawler boat (with outboard motor)
37. Snowflake RU locker
38. Funnel
39. FW hose
40. Anvil
41. 27ft whaler
42. Galley
43. BR vent
44. Snowflake locker
45. Refuse chute
46. Carley float
47. Oerlikon magazine locker
48. ER vent
49. Oerlikon magazine locker
50. Galley coal bunker
51. Oerlikon support
52. ER skylight
53. Vegetable locker
54. Chopping block
55. Beef screen
56. Exhaust from diesel generator
57. Potato locker
58. Inlet to diesel generator
59. Floatanet
60. Floating off buoy

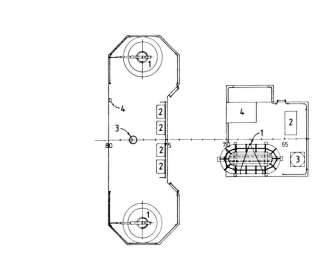

I2/2   I2/3

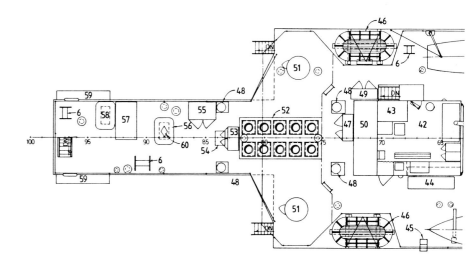

I2/6

I2/4

I2/5

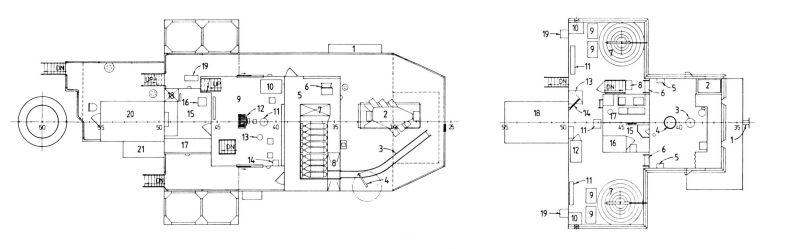

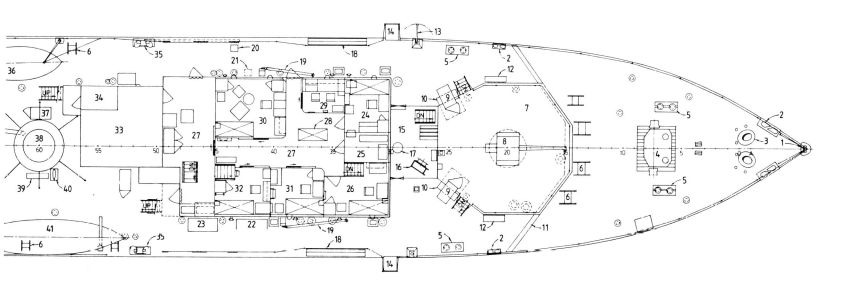

I Modified Flower and Castle class corvettes

I2/7   Plan of upper deck

1. Paint and lamp room
2. Lobby
3. Naval store
4. Chain pipes
5. Stokers' mess
6. Seamen's mess
7. CPOs' and POs' mess
8. WC
9. Officers' bath room
10. Shower
11. Ammunition trunk
12. Cabin
13. Passage
14. ERAs' mess
15. Ward room
16. Ward room pantry
17. Fan flat
18. Boiler room casing
19. Engine room casing
20. Diesel generator room
21. DC workshop
22. CPOs' and POs' washplace
23. Regulating office
24. Issue room
25. Sick bay
26. Ablution cabin
27. Crew's heads
28. Ward room store
29. Steward and cooks' mess
30. Canteen
31. Decontamination store
32. Crew's washplace
33. Sand box
34. Wash deck locker
35. Refuse bins
36. Bollard
37. Life saving net
38. Accommodation ladder
39. Reel
40. DC stowage
41. DC thrower
42. Davit
43. DC chute
44. Smoke float
45. WT trunk

I2/8   Plan of lower deck

1. Fore peak
2. Chain locker
3. A/S instrument room
4. Canteen store
5. Provision room
6. Seamen's mess
7. LP room
8. Gyro compass room
9. 20-ton pump
10. Boiler room
11. Oil fuel tank
12. Engine room
13. Electricians' and engineers' workshop
14. Gunners' store
15. Lobby
16. Naval store
17. Paymaster's store
18. Provision room
19. Steering gear compartment

I2/9   Plan of hold

1. Fore peak
2. Store
3. A/S compartment
4. Fresh water tank
5. 4in magazine
6. Cold room
7. Lobby
8. Refrigeration machinery
9. Fuel oil tank
10. Oerlikon magazine
11. Squid projectile room
12. Reserve feed water tank
13. Engine room
14. Main feed water tank
15. Spirit room
16. Engineers' store
17. Gland compartment

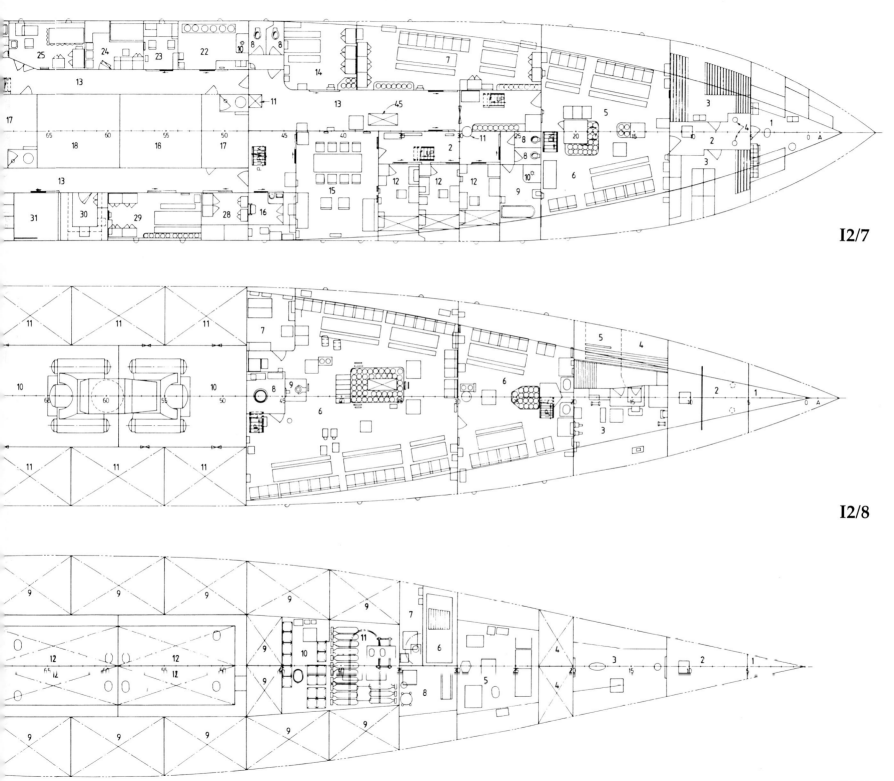

SOURCES

Sources

Admiralty *Handbook & Drill for 20mm Oerlikon Machine Gun* London, 1941

— *Manual of Seamanship* (Volume I) London, 1937

Abelsen, Frank *Marinens Fartøyer 1939–1945 og deres Skjebne* Oslo, 1986

Campbell, John *Naval Weapons of World War II* London, 1985

Costello, John & Hughes, Terry *The Battle of the Atlantic* London, 1977

Easton, Alan *50 North: Canada's Atlantic Battleground* Toronto, 1966

Elliott, Peter *Allied Escort Ships of World War II* London, 1983

— *Allied Minesweeping in World War II* Cambridge, 1979

German, Tony *The Sea is at our Gates: The History of the Canadian Navy* Toronto, 1990

Gröner, Erich (ed Jung, D & Maass, M) *Die deutschen Kriegsschiffe 1815–1945* Koblenz, 1982 (continuing); also available as *German Warships 1815–1945* London, 1990 (continuing)

Harland, John *Catchers and Corvettes: The Steam Whalecatcher in Peace and War 1860–1960* Rotherfield, 1992

— 'The Design of the Flower Class Corvette and its Relationship to the Whaler *Southern Pride* of 1936' *Warship 1991* London, 1991

Hodges, Peter *Royal Navy Warship Camouflage 1939–45* London, 1971

Lamb, James *The Corvette Navy* Toronto, 1977

Lenton, Trevor *American Gunboats and Minesweepers* New York, 1974

Lenton, Trevor & Colledge, James *Warships of World War II* London, 1973

Lynch, Thomas *Canada's Flowers: A History of the Corvettes of Canada 1939–1945* Halifax, 1981

Macpherson, Ken & Burgess, John *The Ships of Canada's Naval Forces 1910–1981* Toronto, 1981

Macpherson, Ken & Milner, Marc *Flower Class Corvettes of Canada* St Catherines, Ontario, 1993

Milner, Marc *The North Atlantic Run: The Royal Canadian Navy and the Battle for the Convoys* Toronto, 1985

Preston, Anthony & Raven, Alan *Flower Class Corvettes* London, 1973

RINA (transactions) *Selected Papers on British Warship Design in World War II* London, 1983

Roberts, Leslie *Canada and the War at Sea* Montreal, 1944

Waters, John M *Bloody Winter* New York, 1967